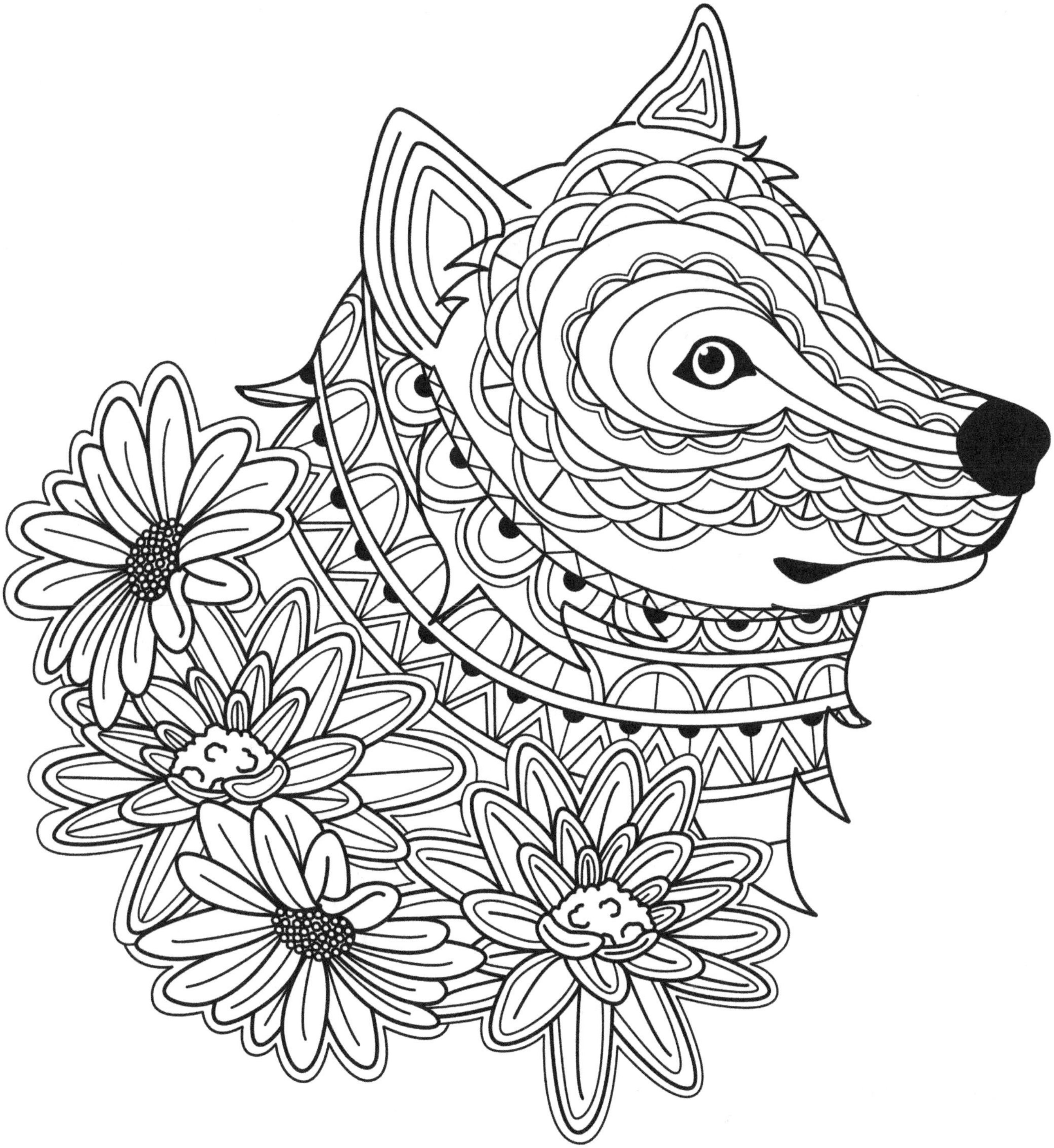

ISBN: 978-1523452767
Illustrated by:
    Mandala & Caricature Illustration
    Joshua Lazana Lagman and Jade Villaremo

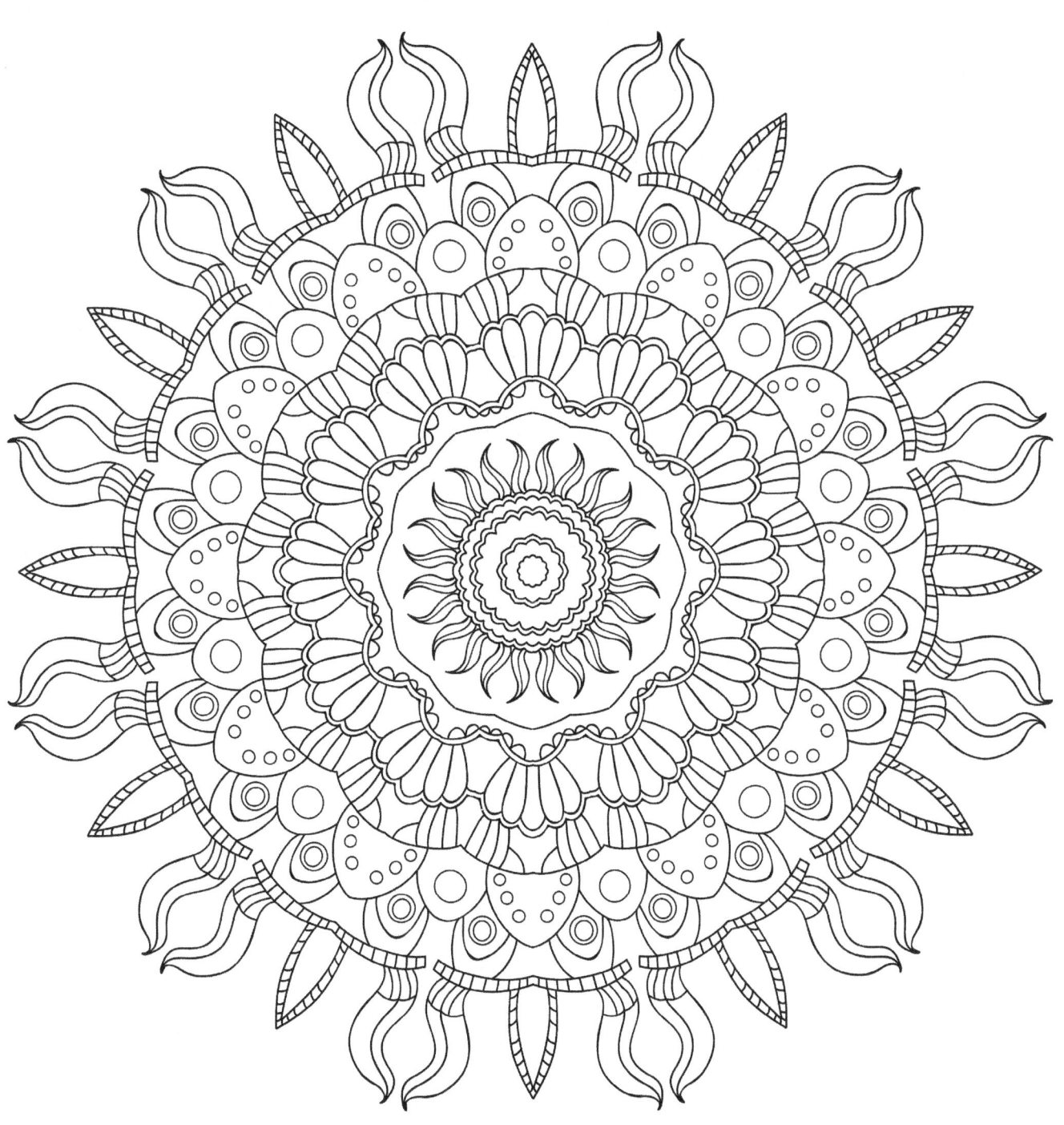

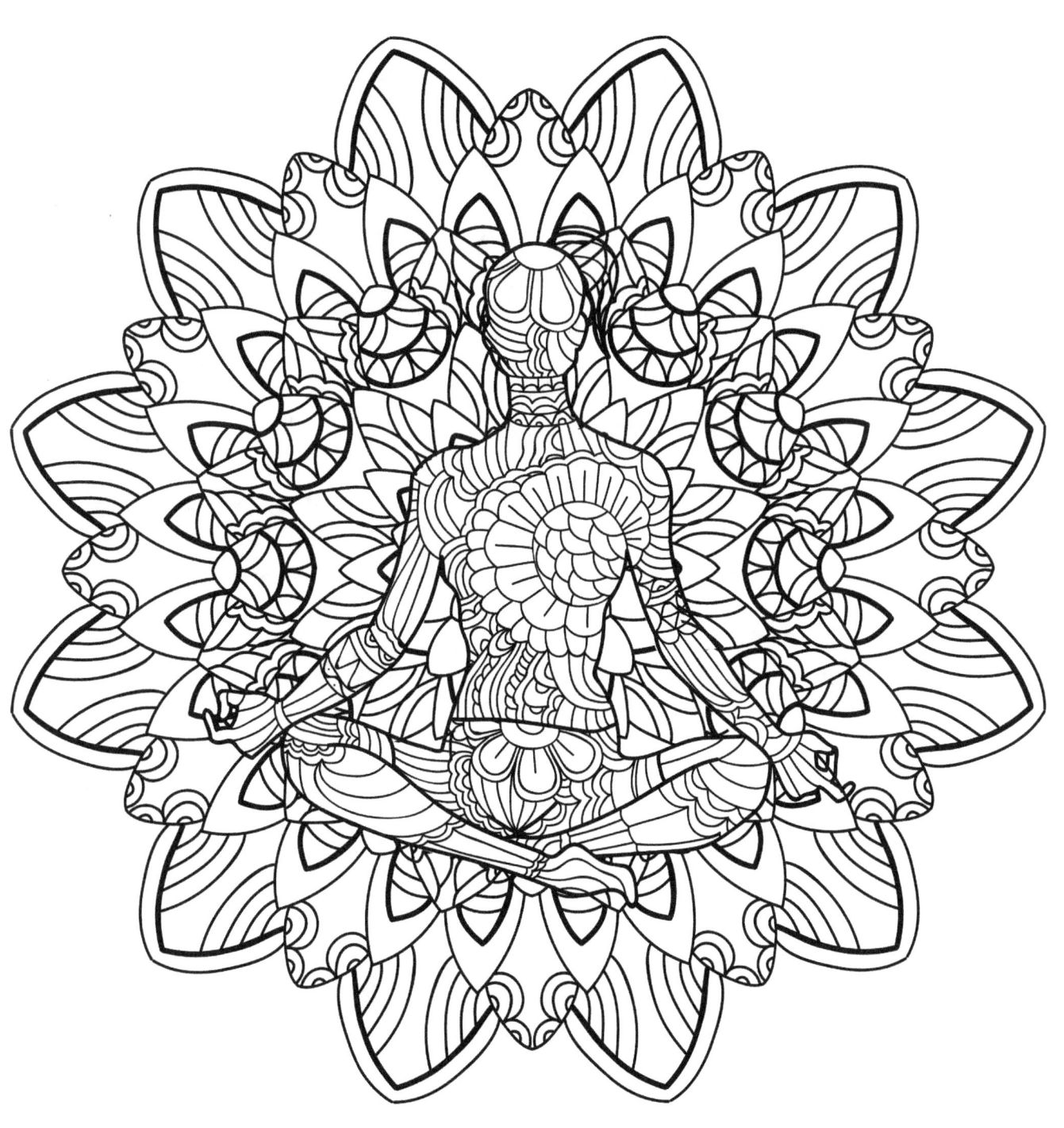

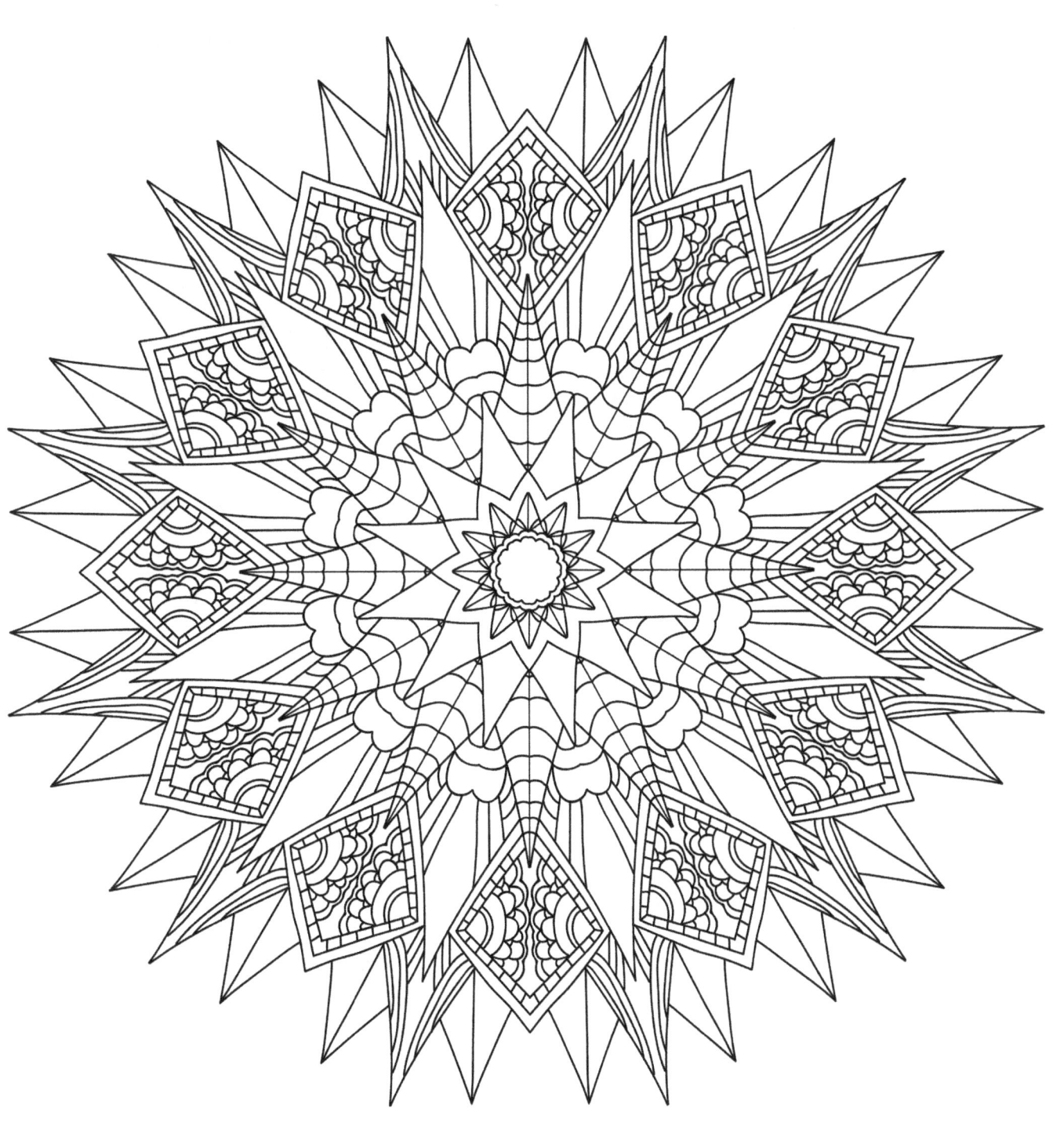

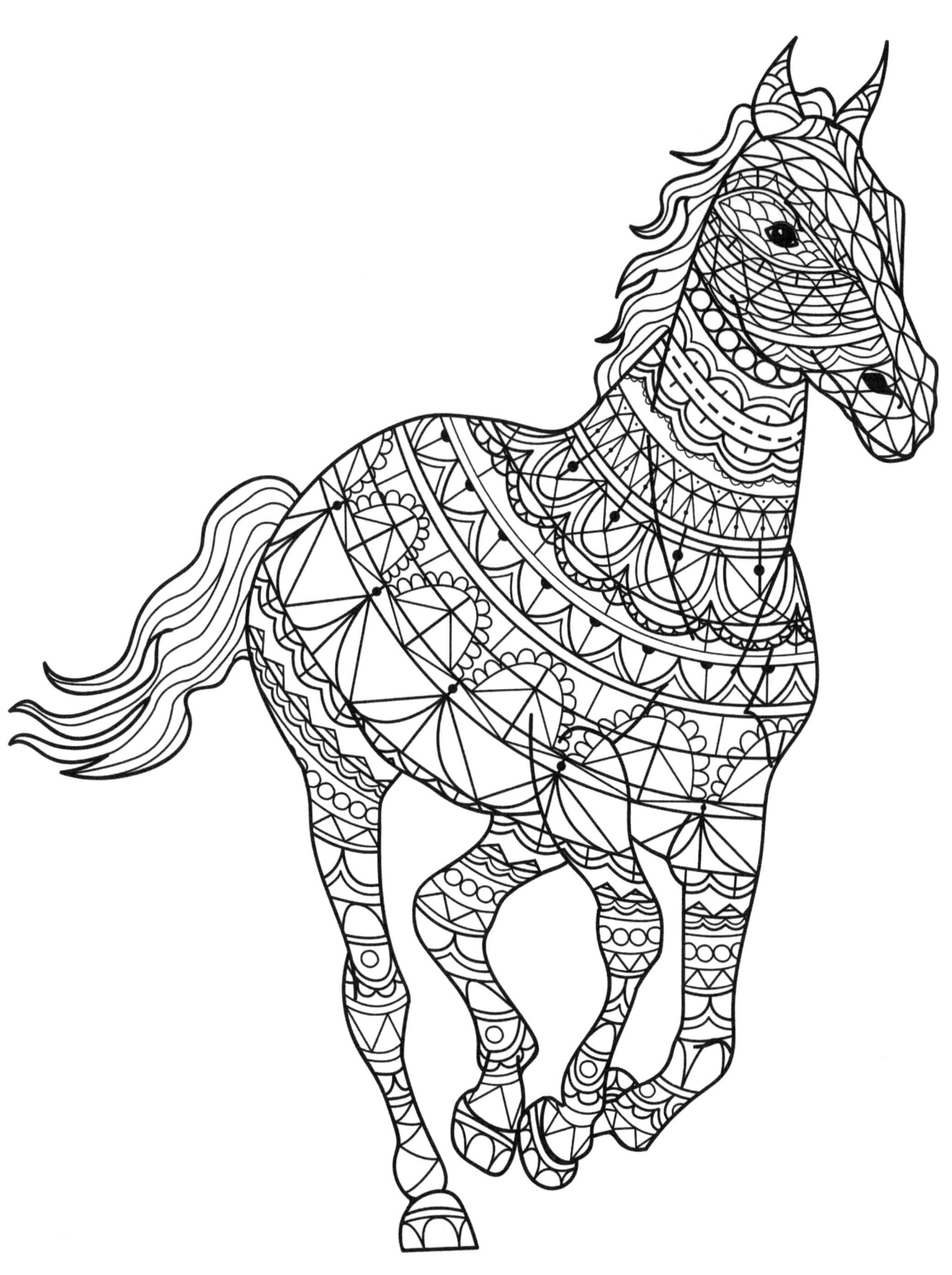

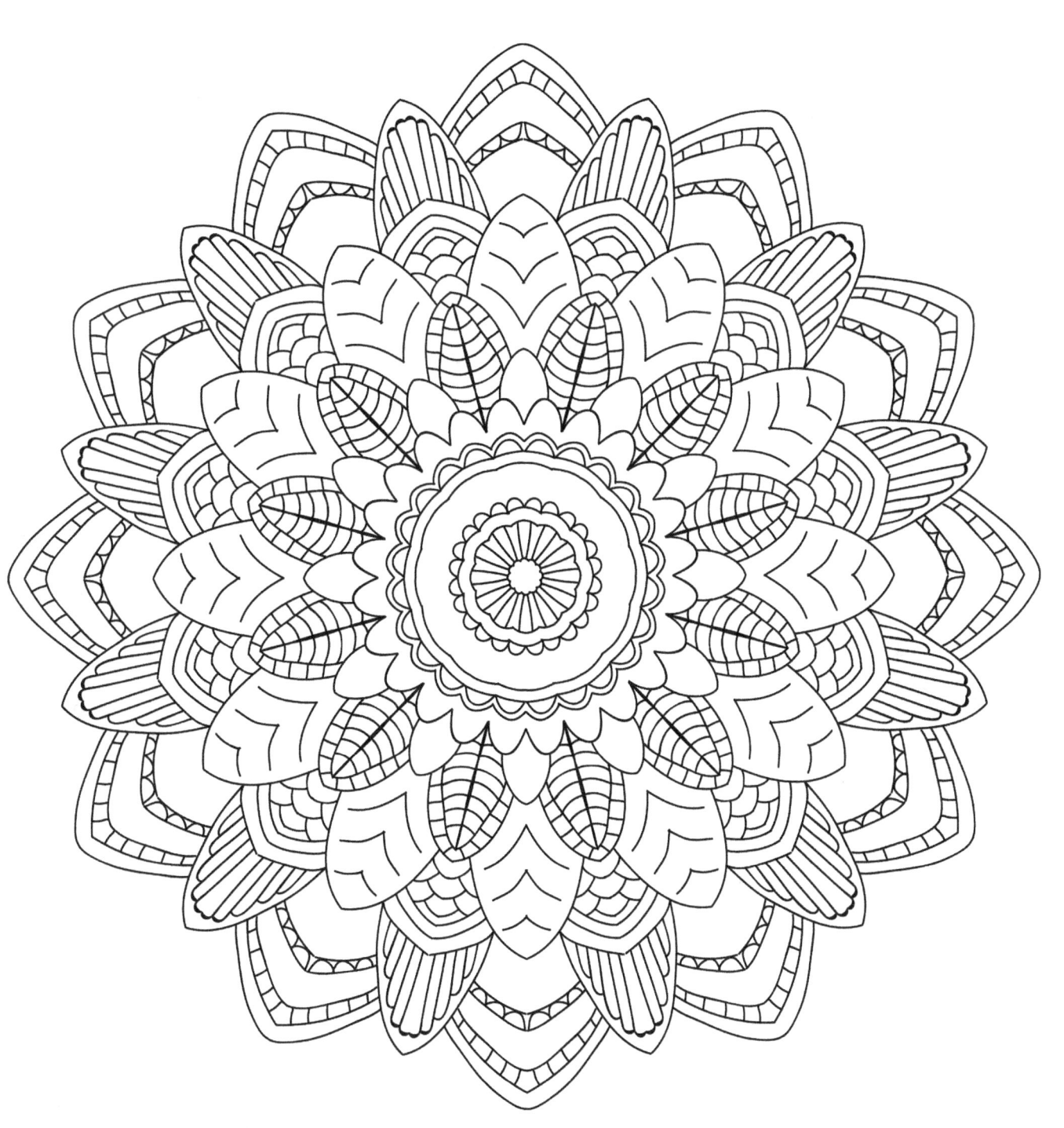

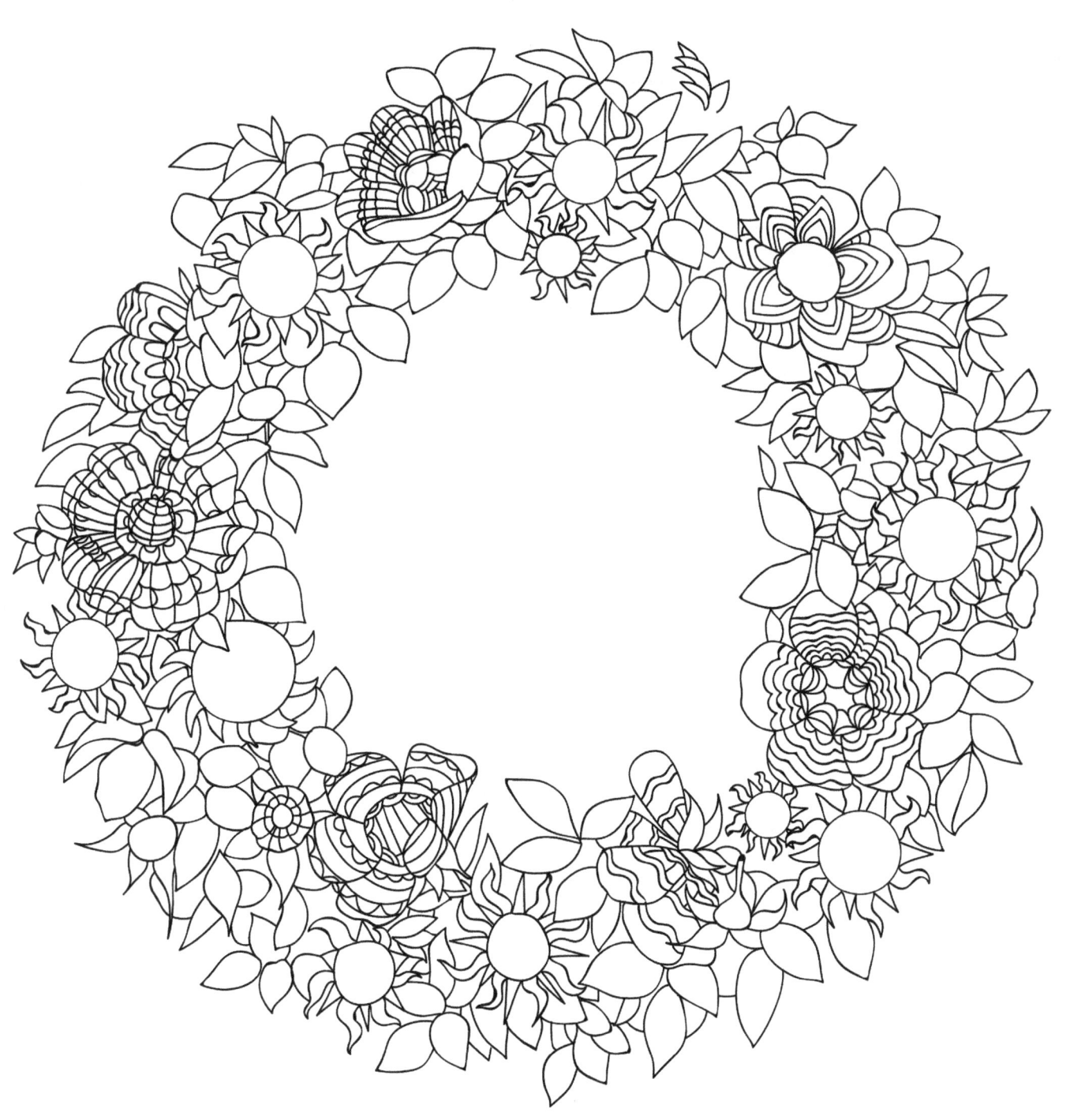

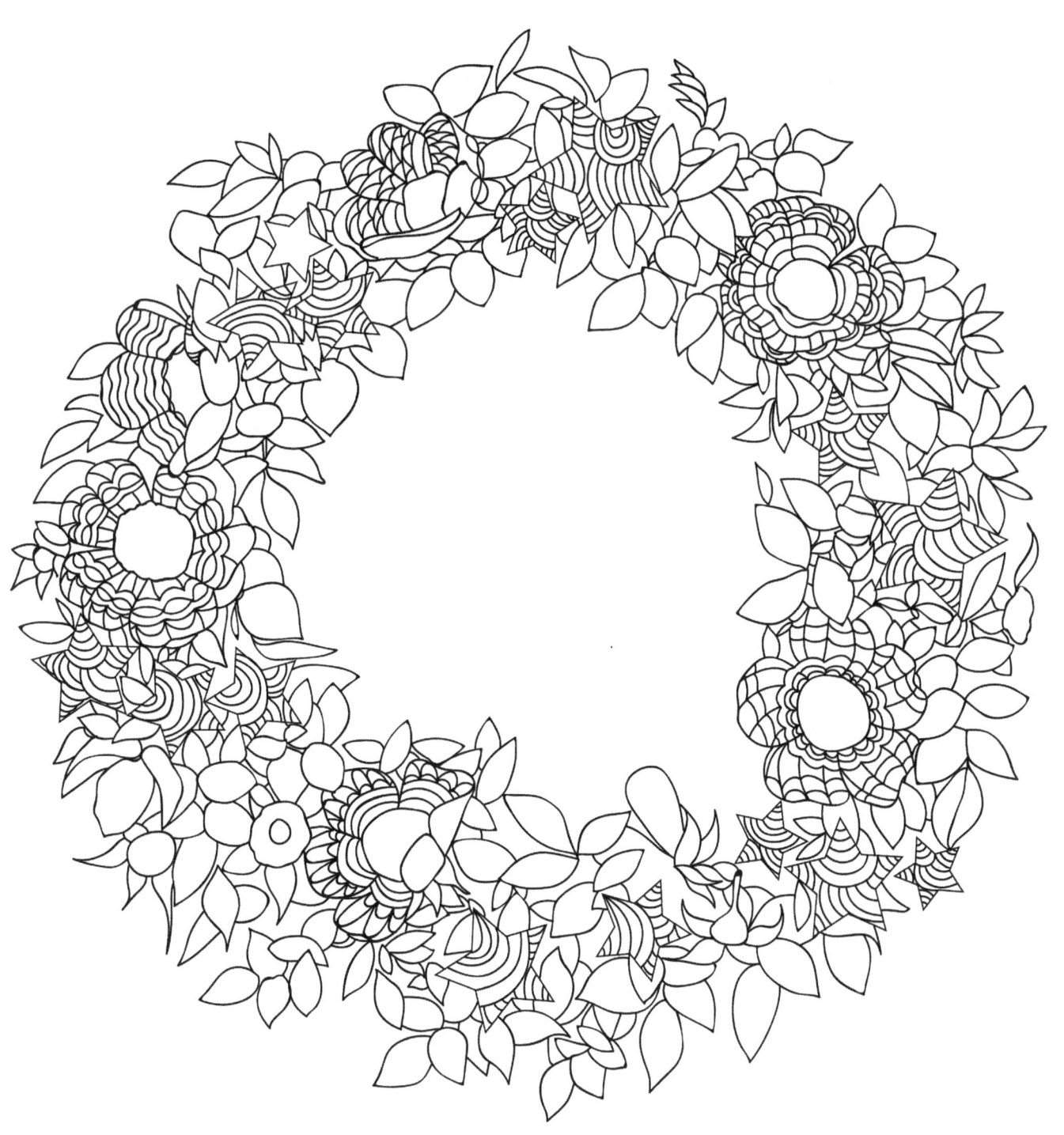

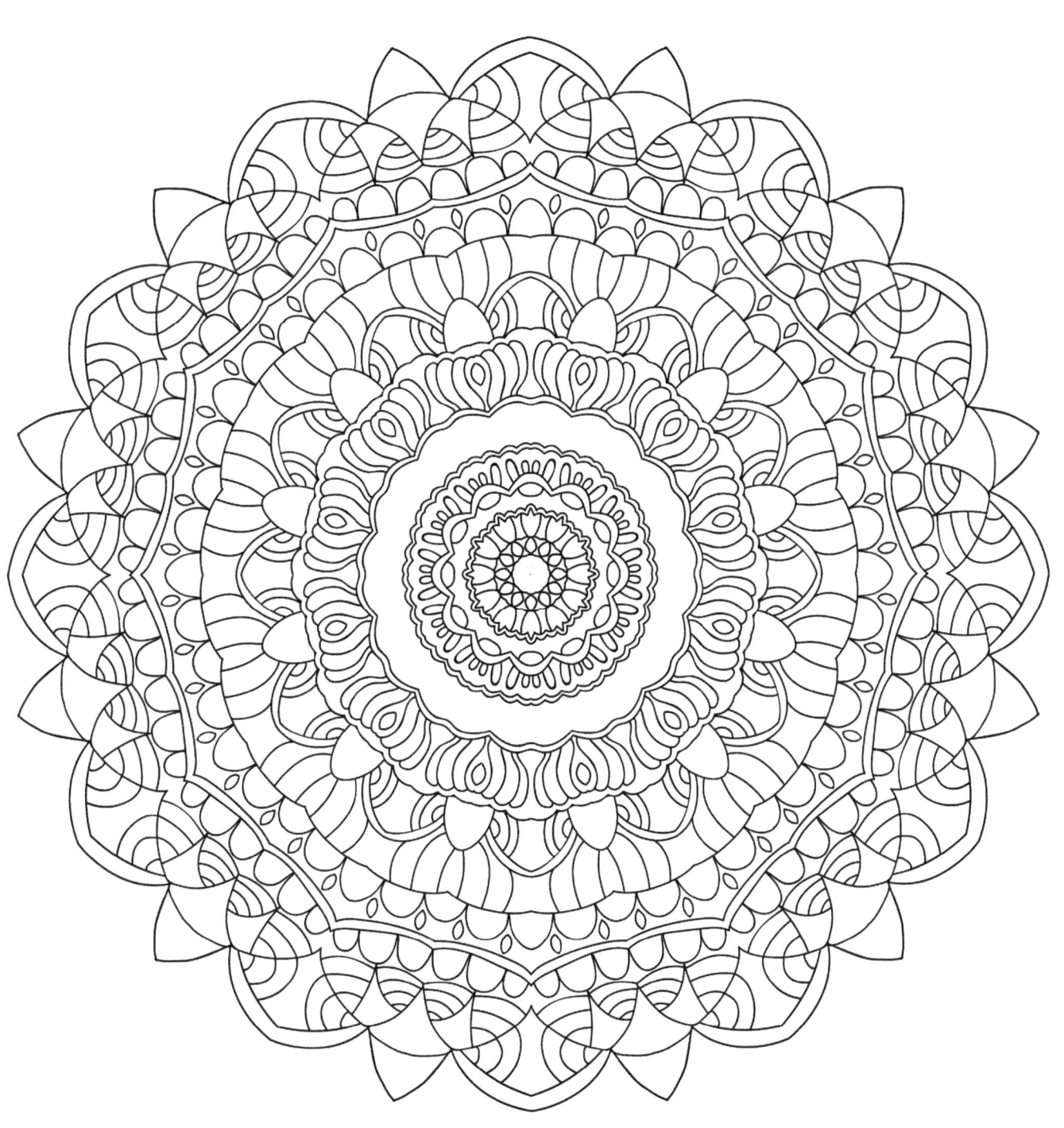

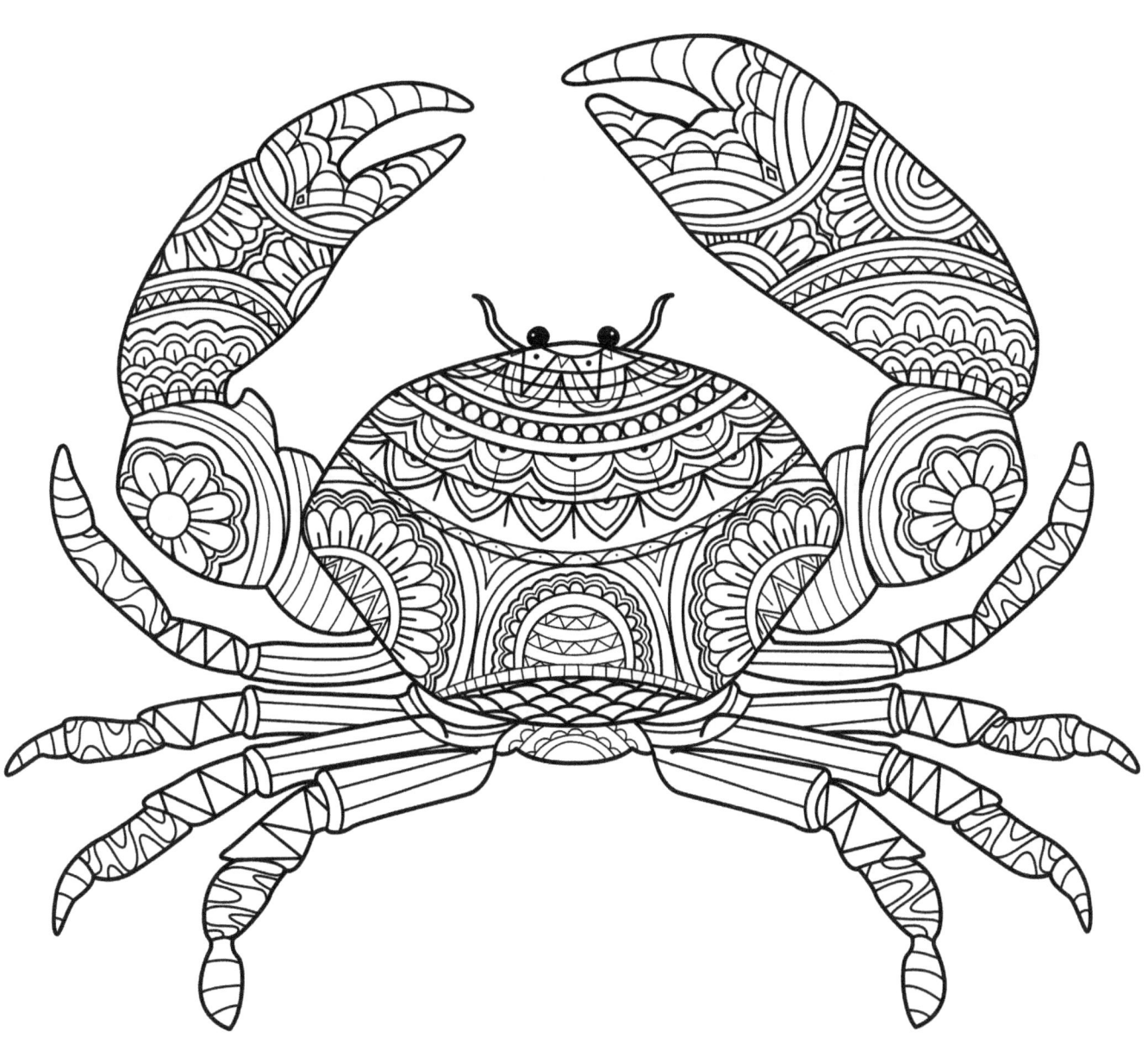

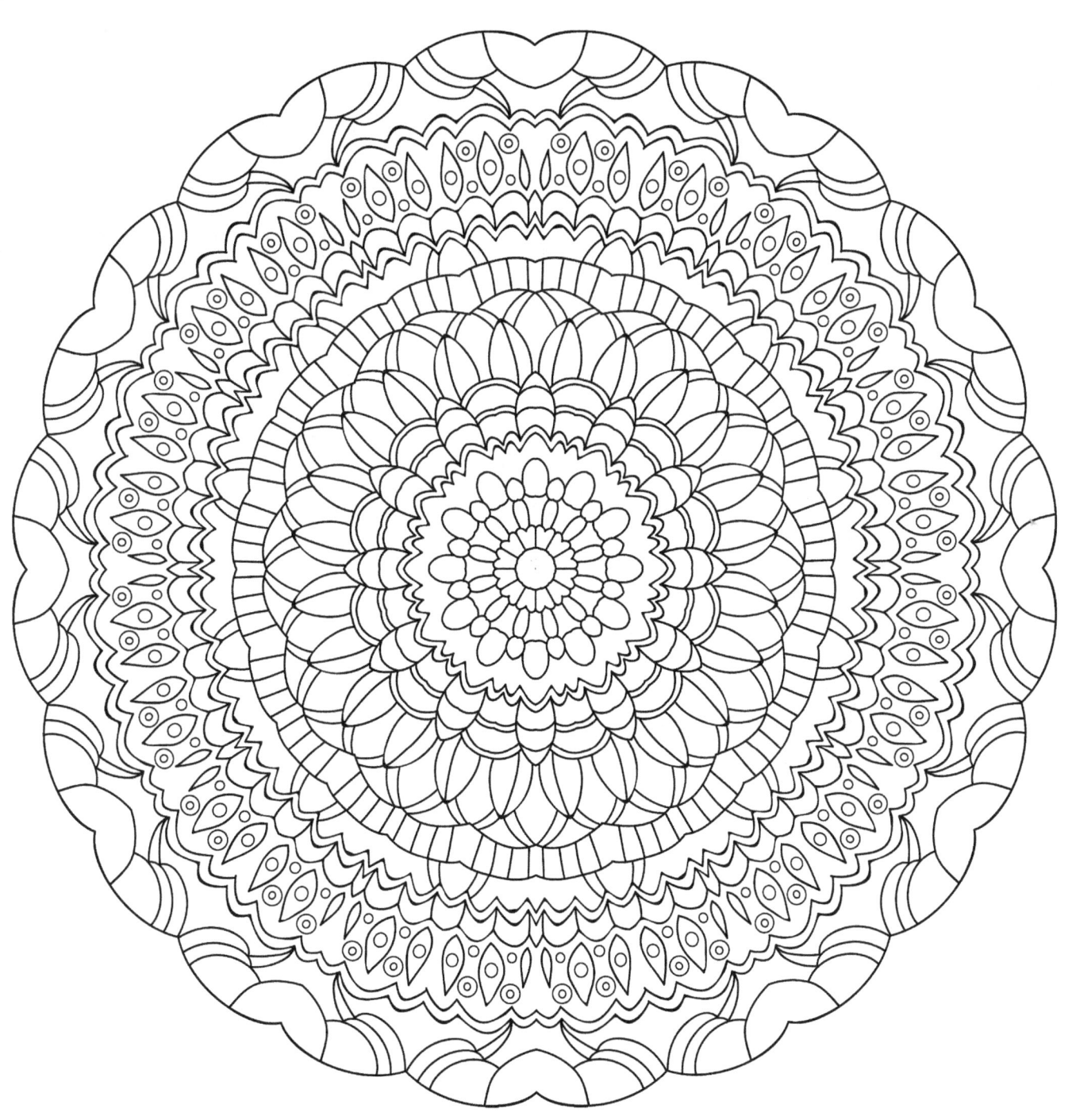

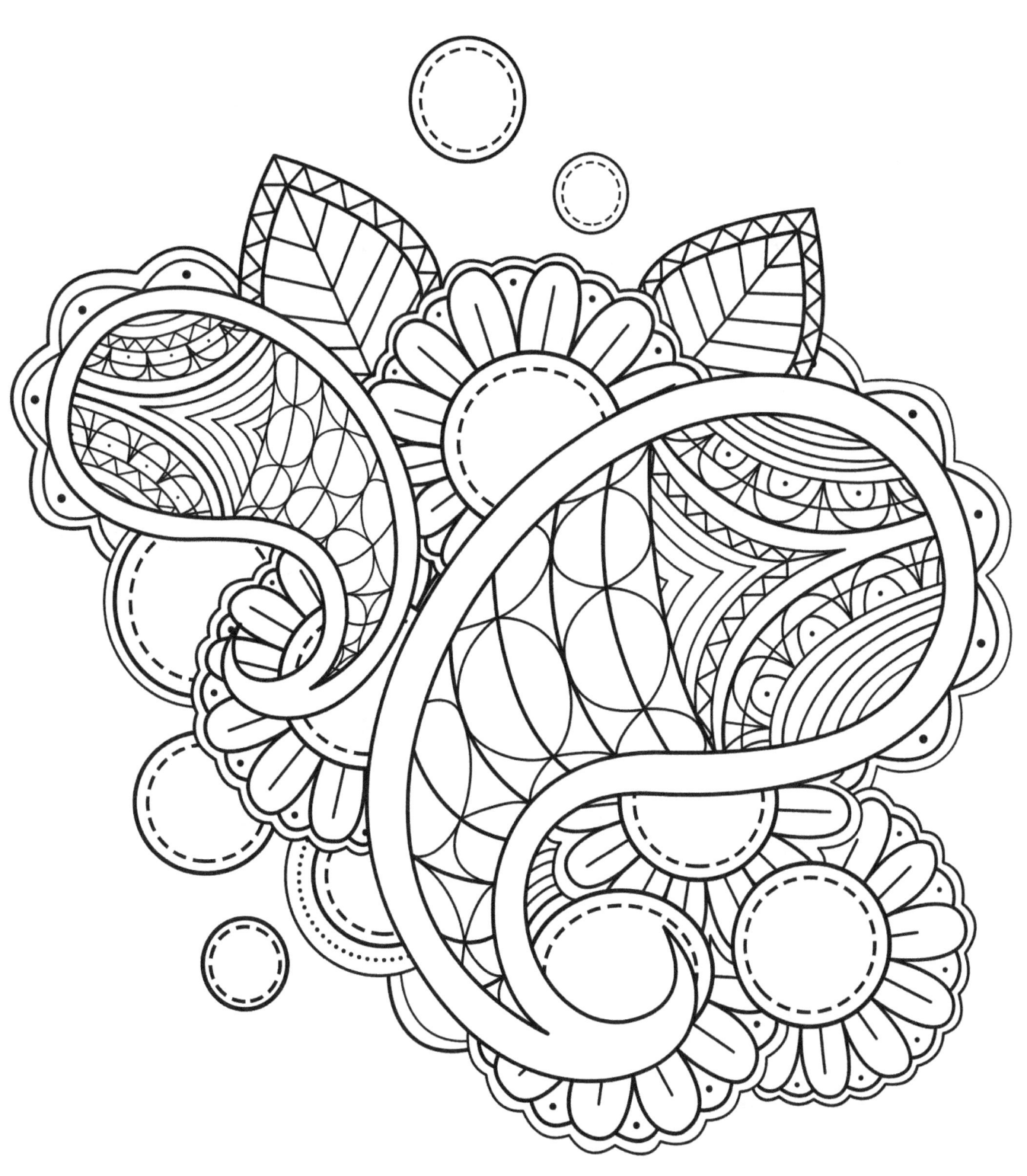

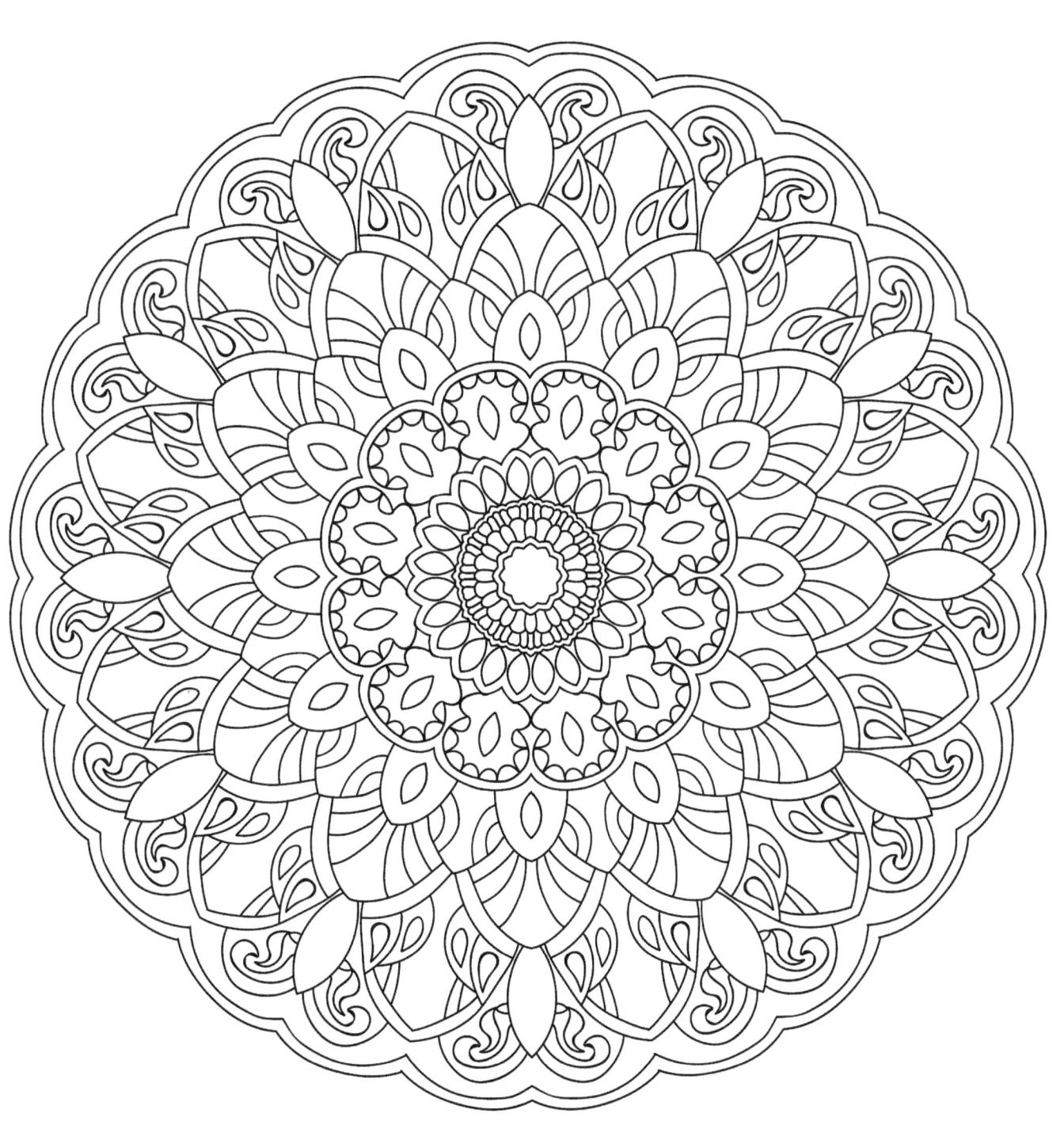

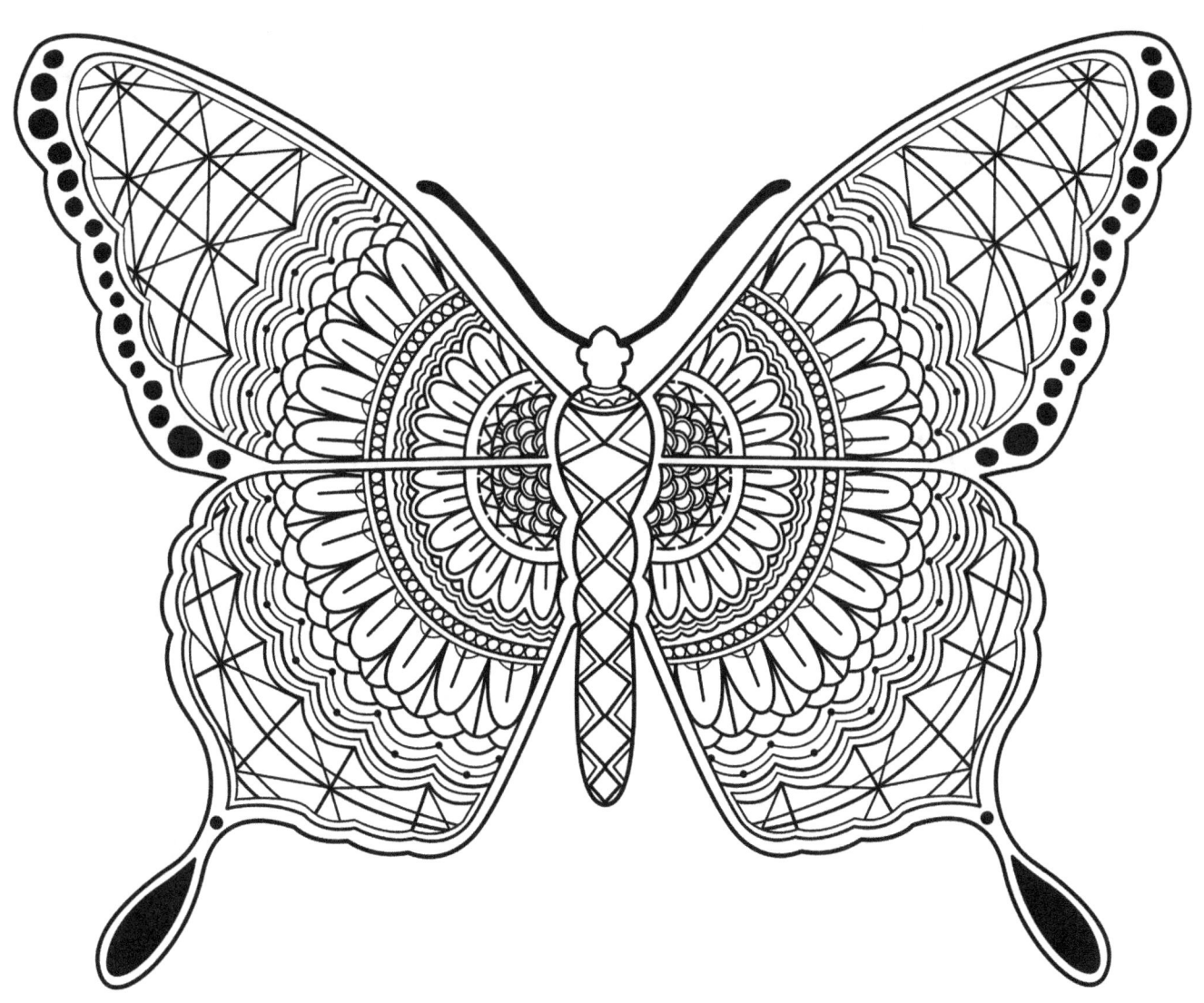

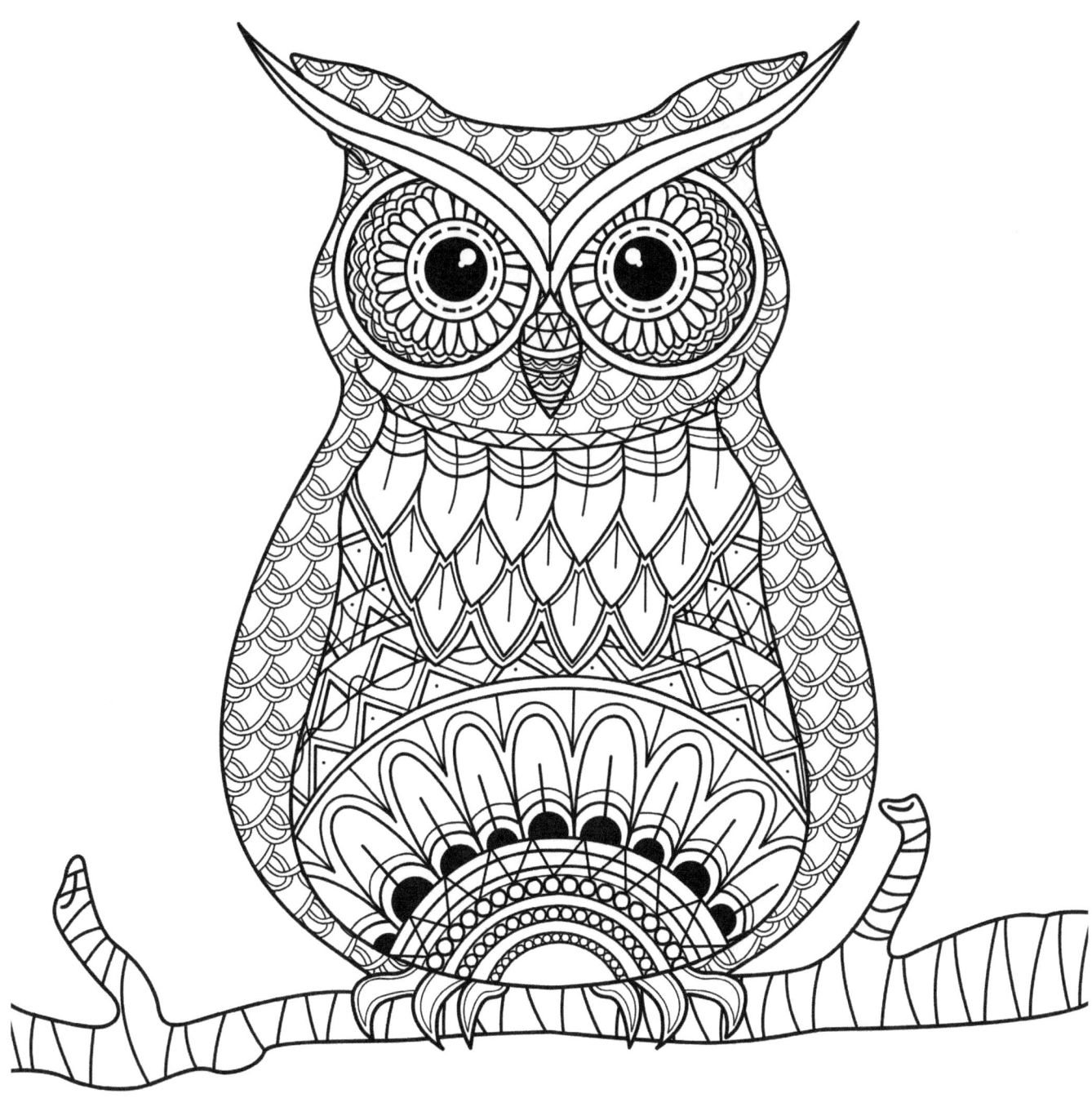

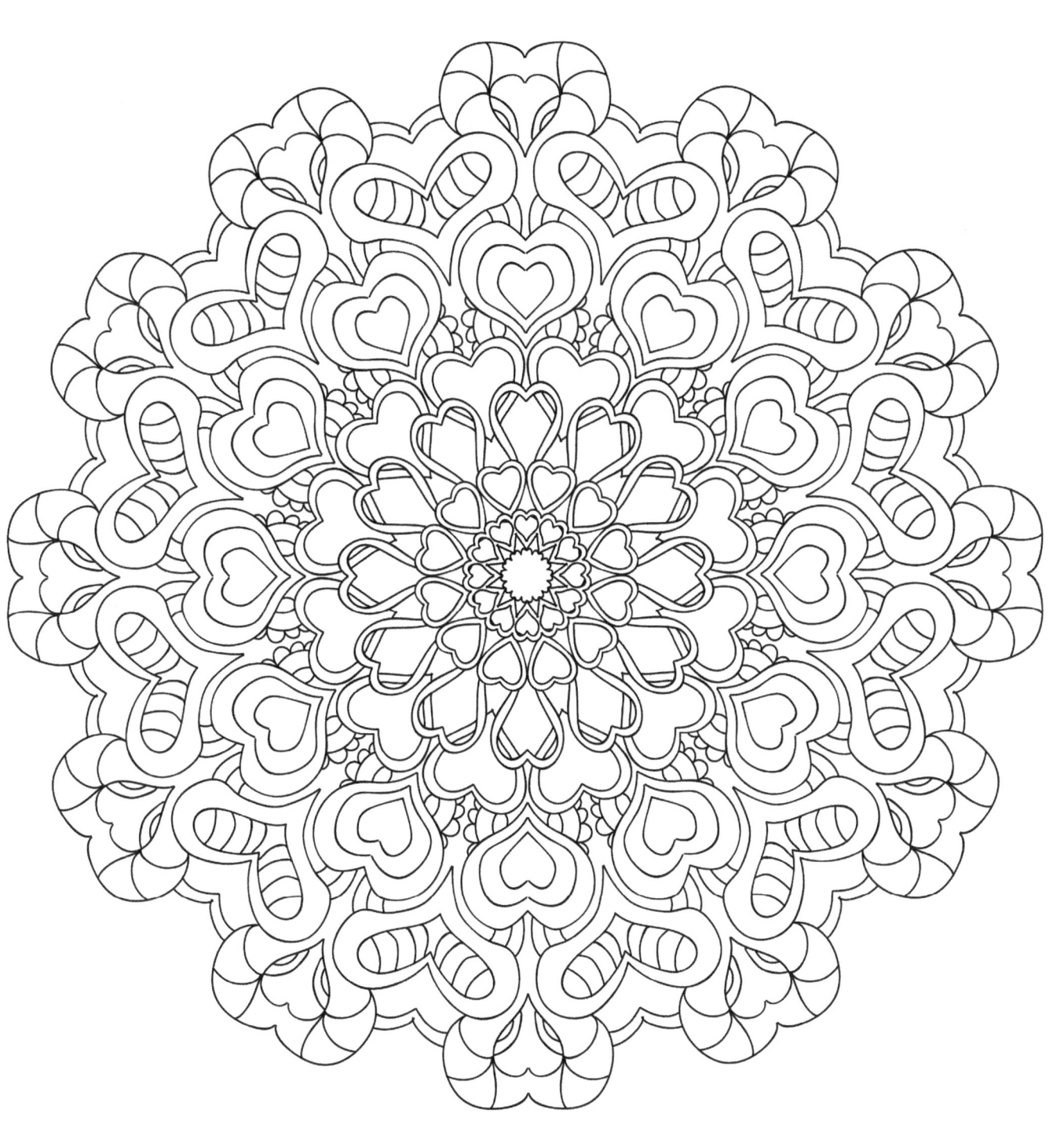

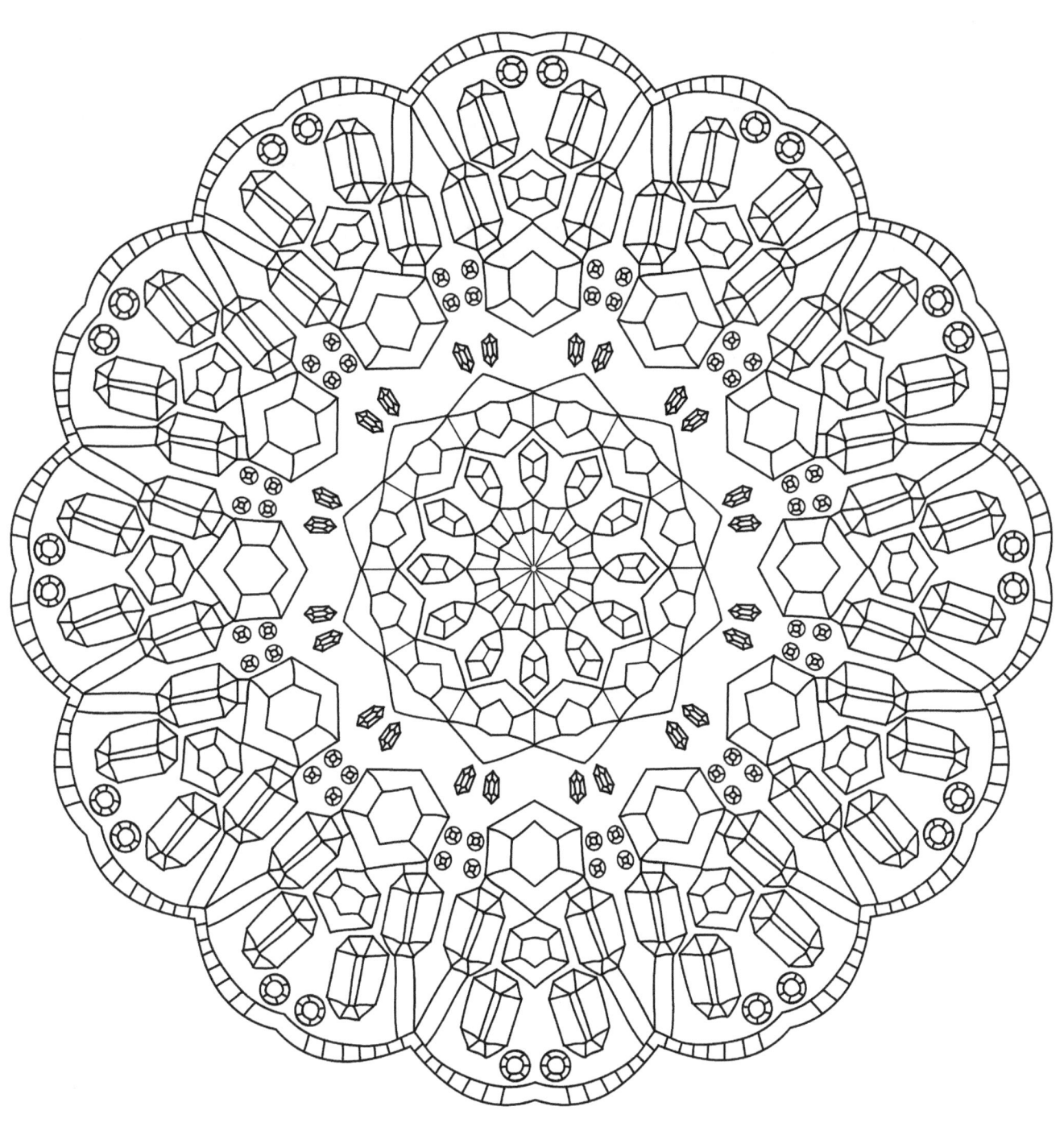

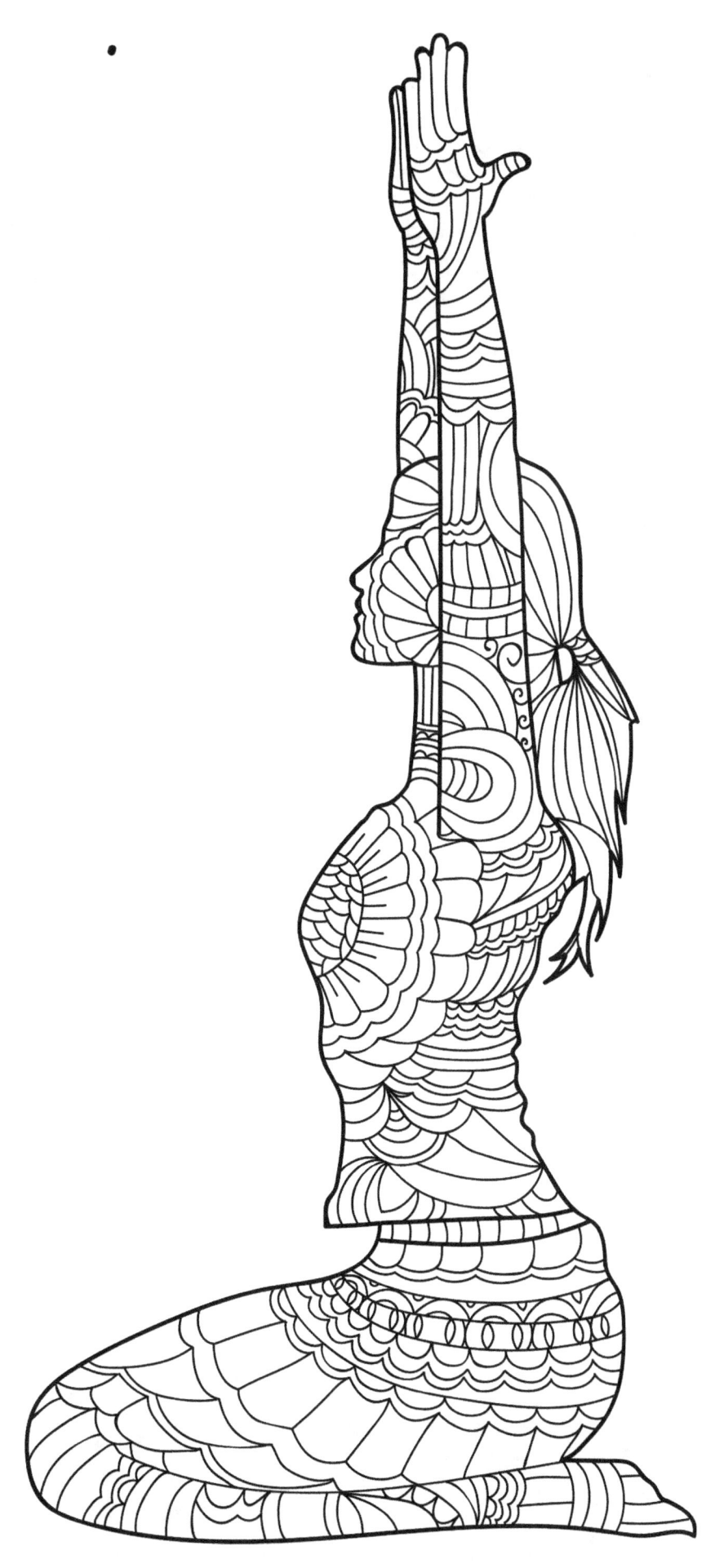

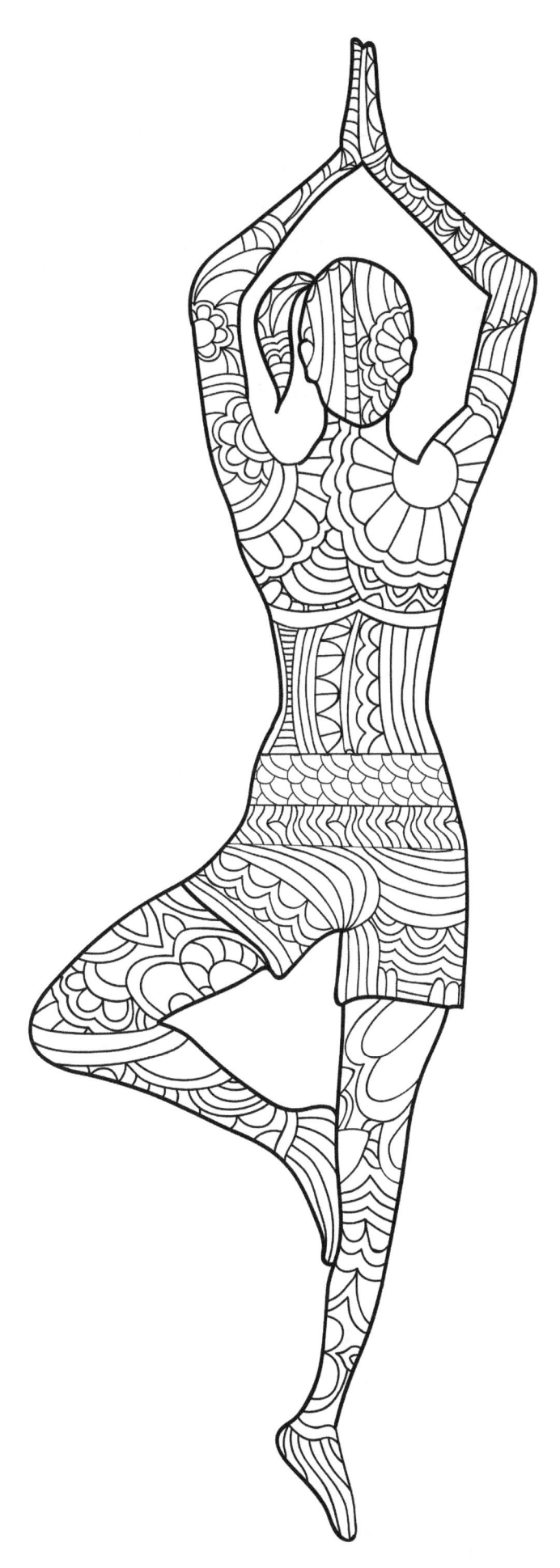

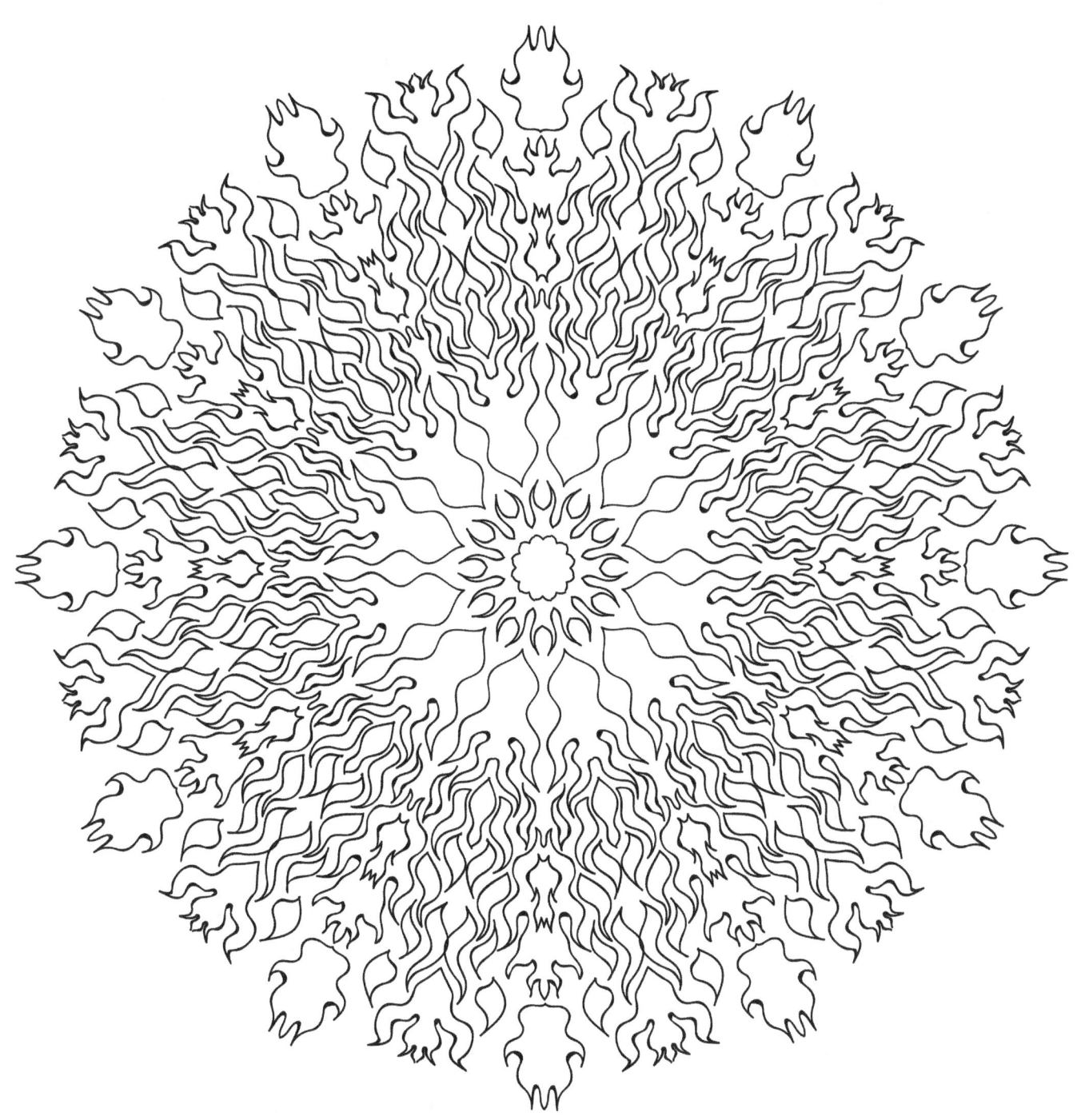

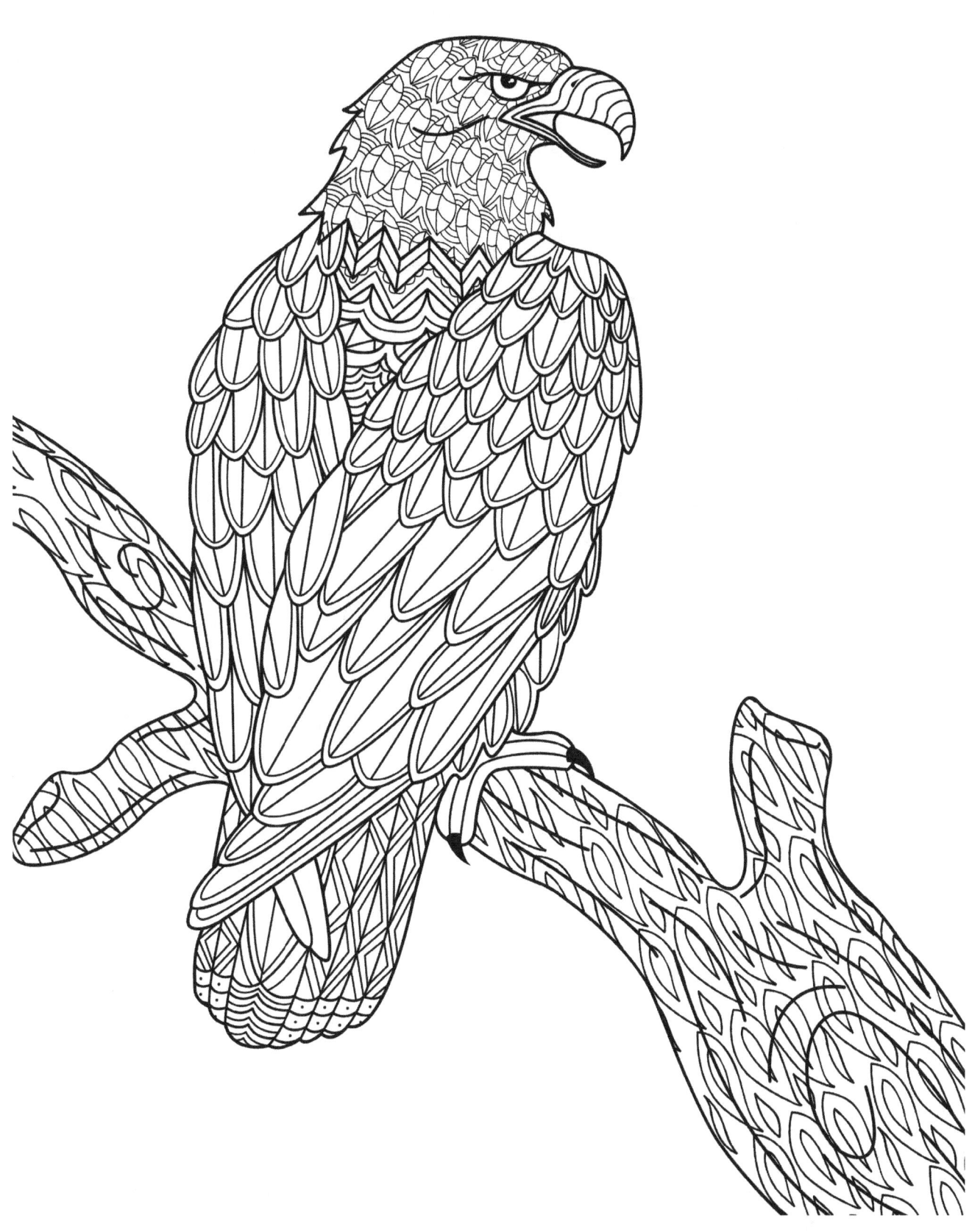

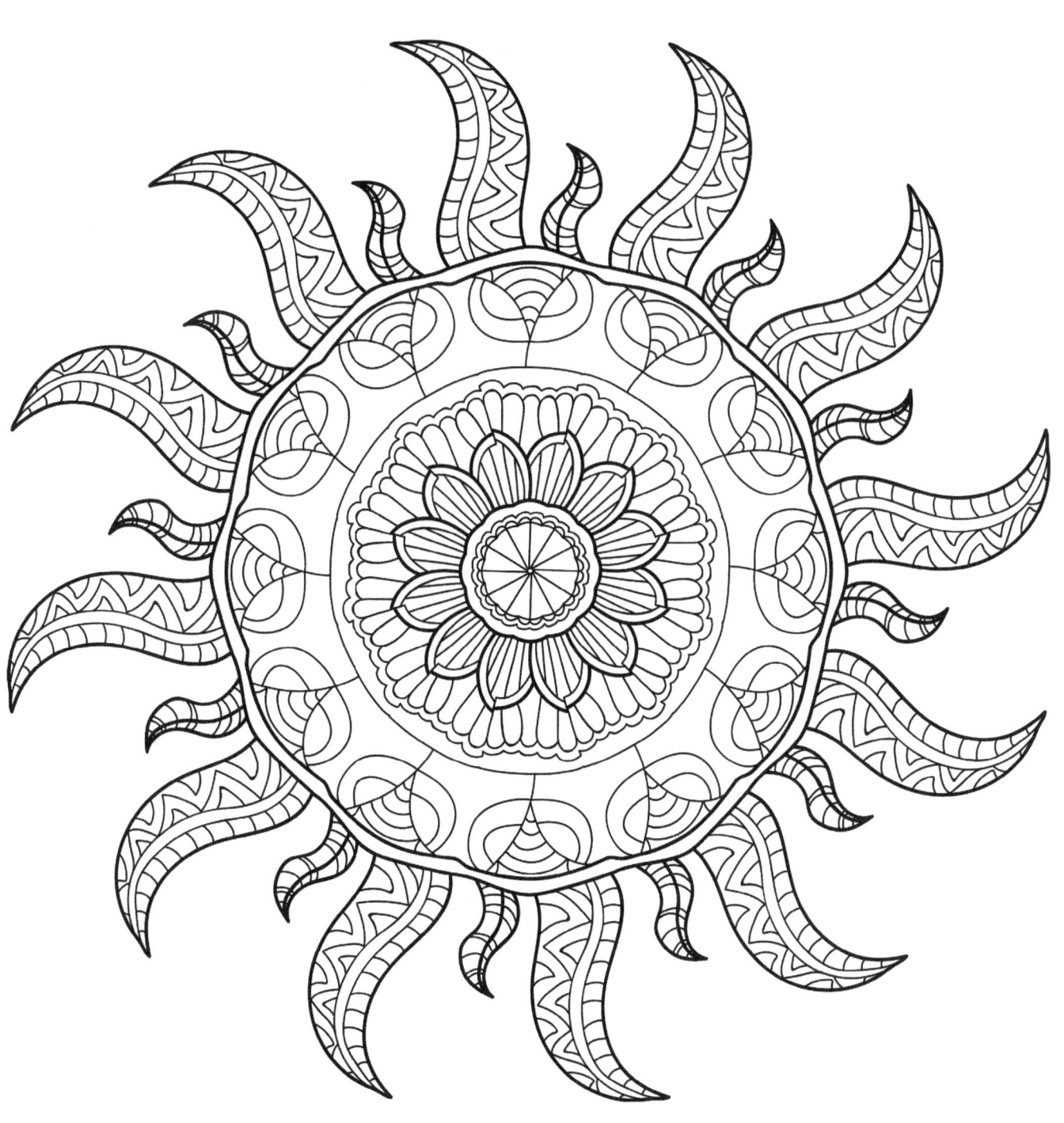

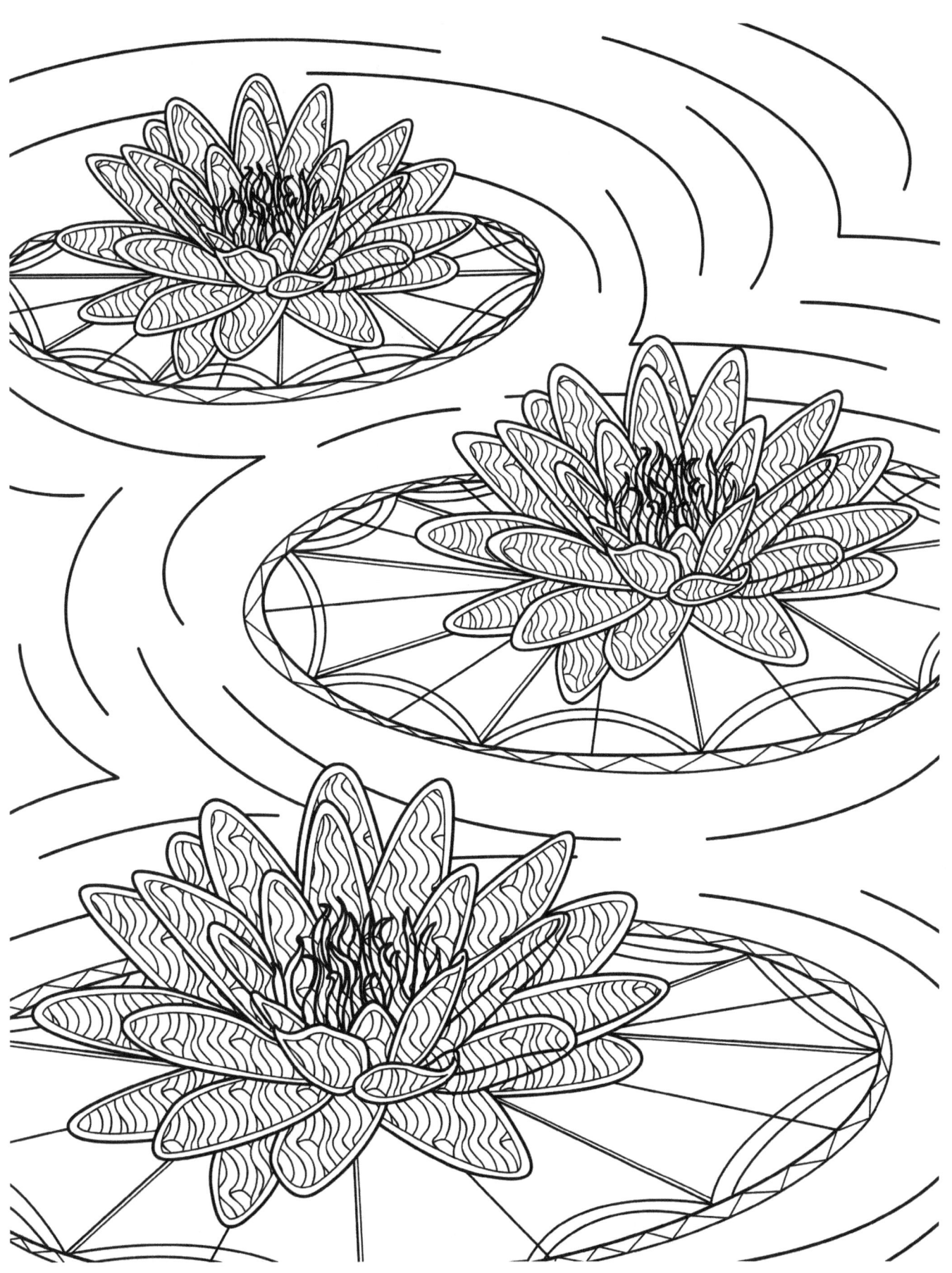

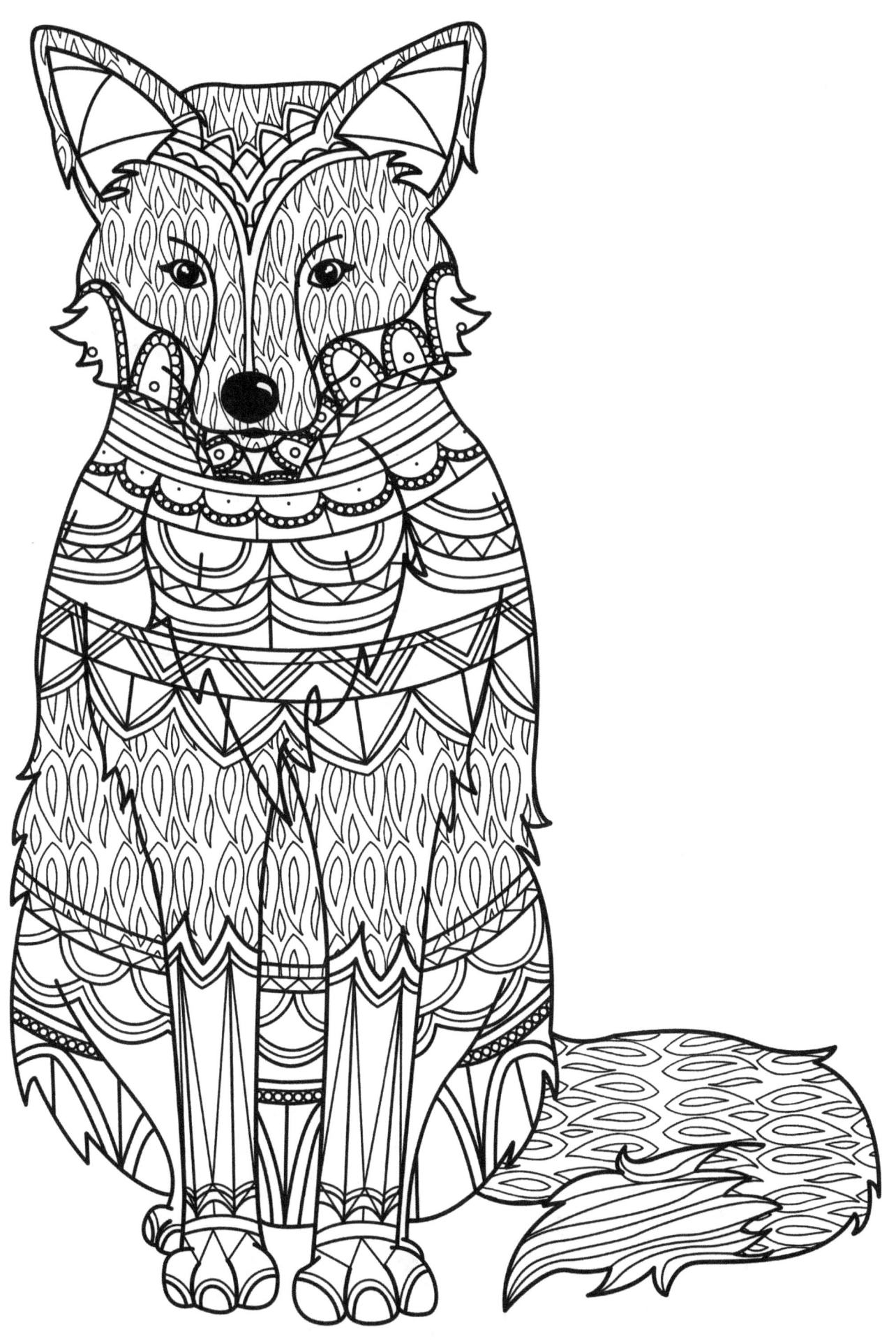

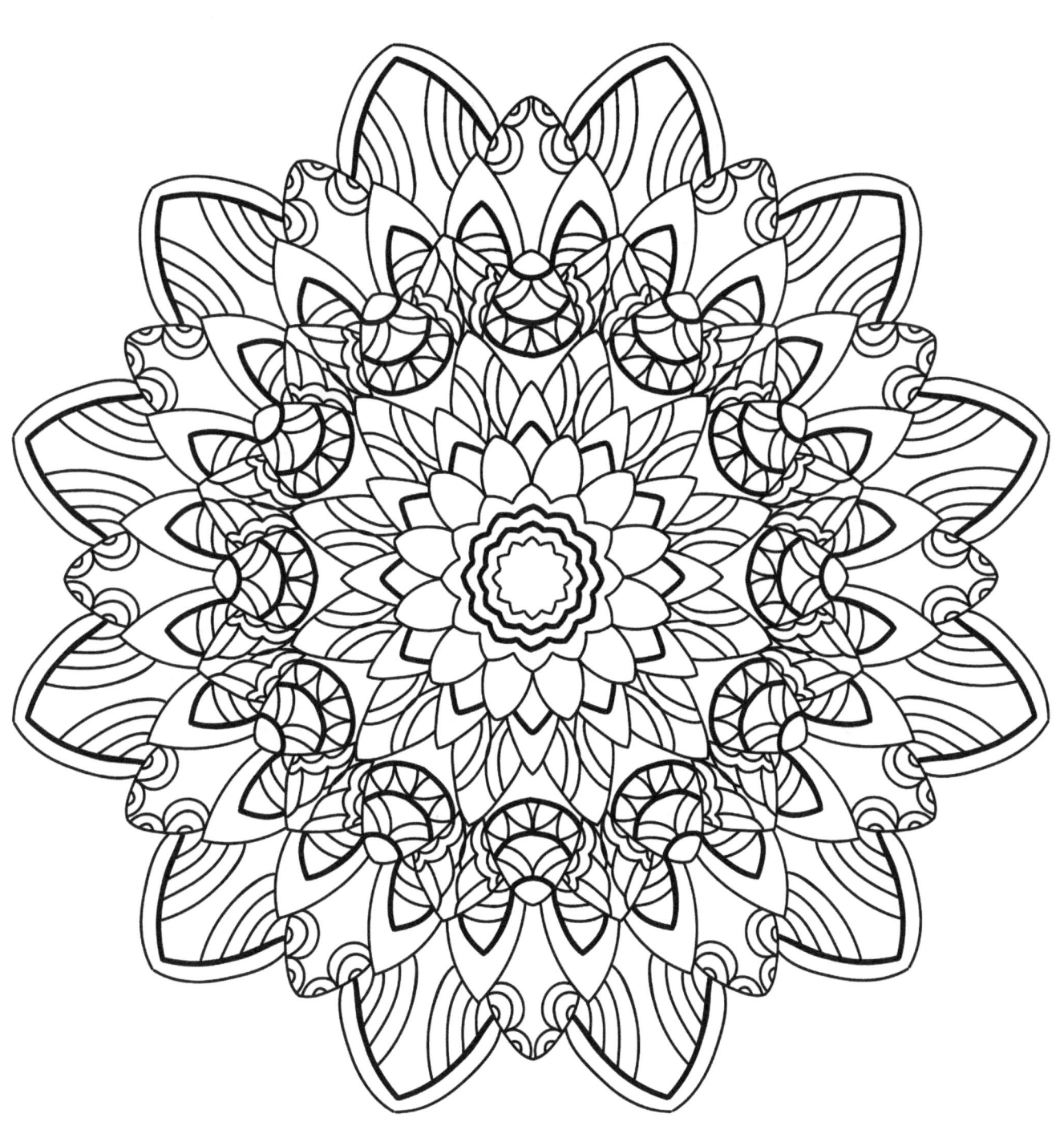

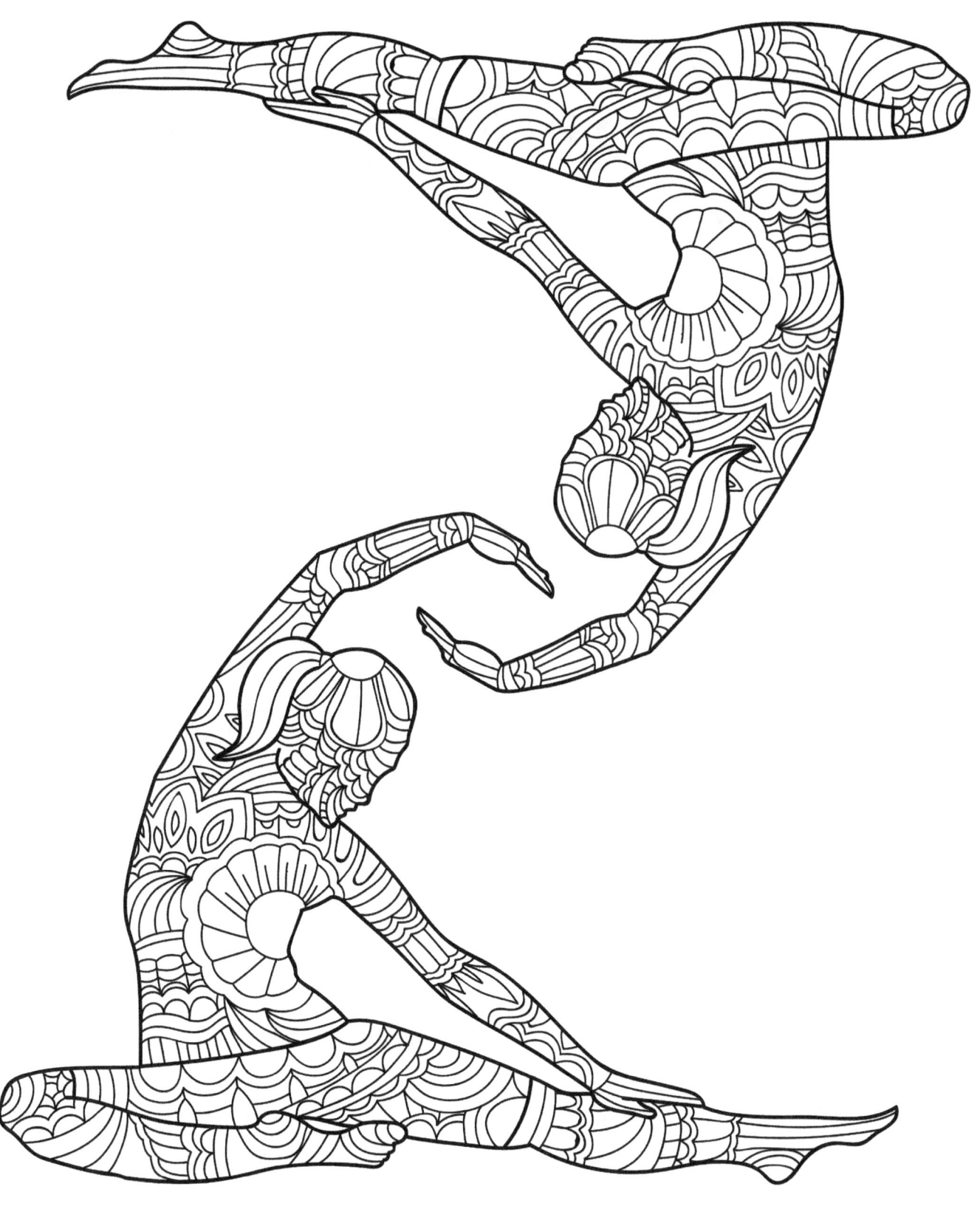

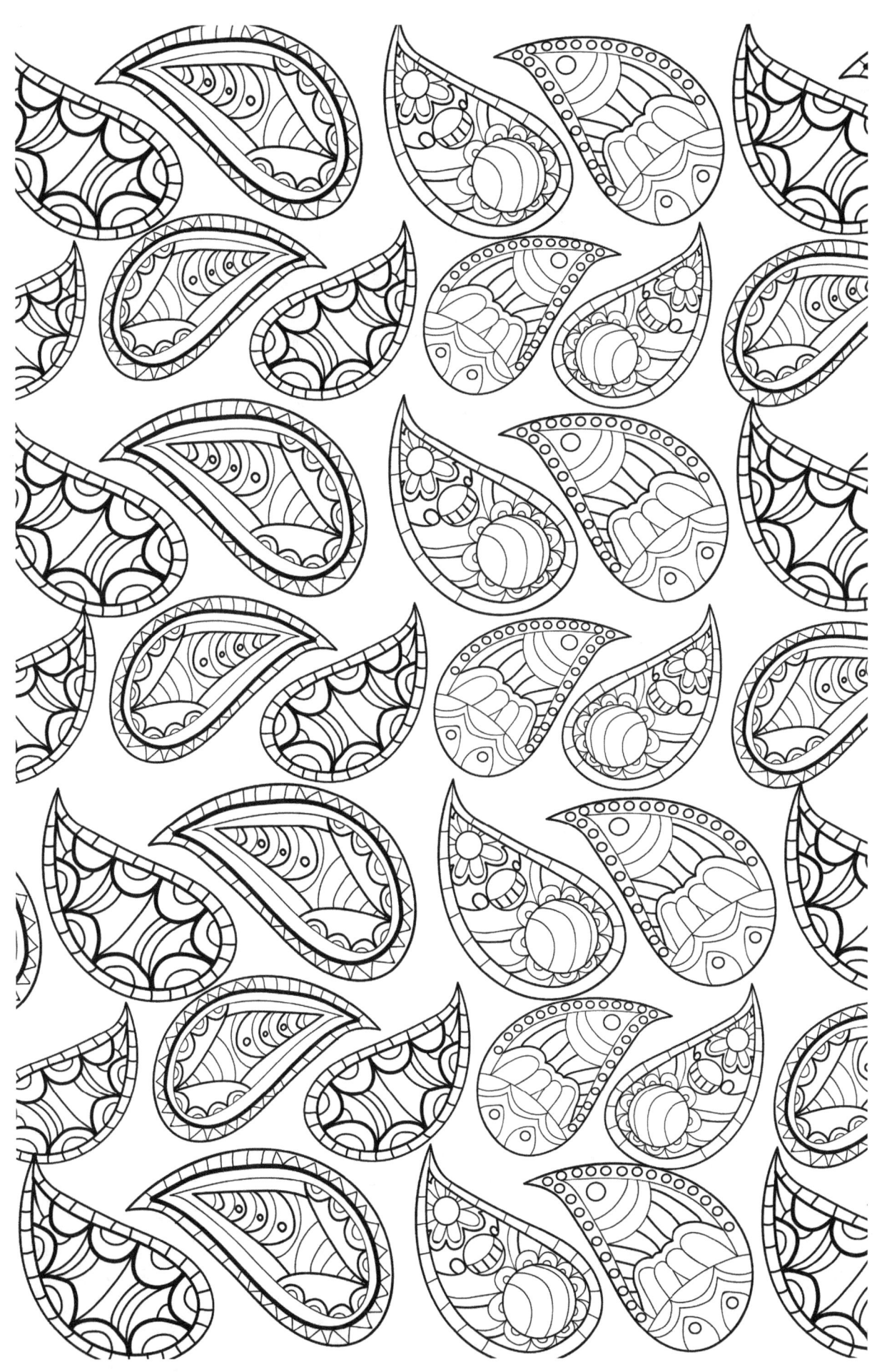

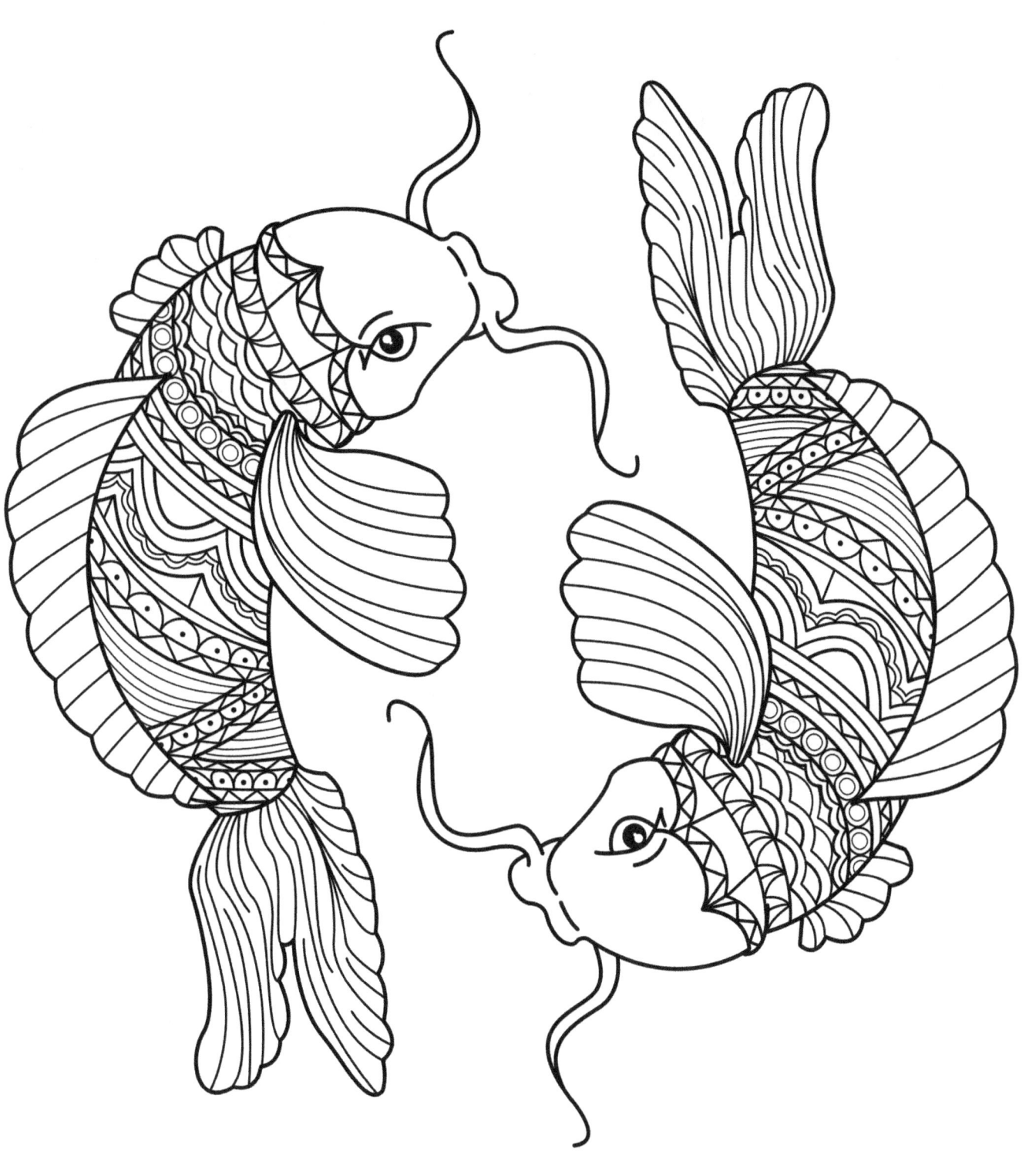

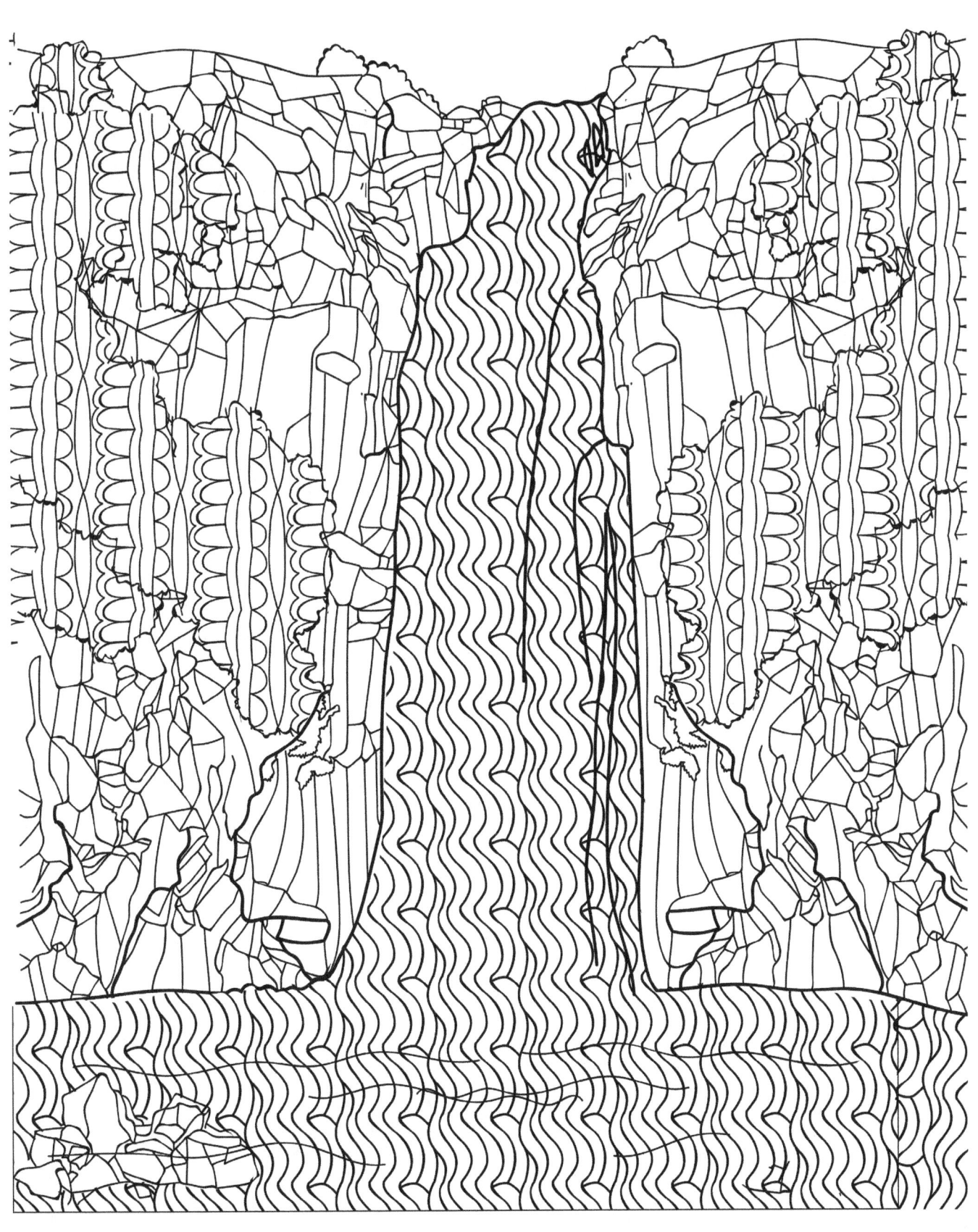

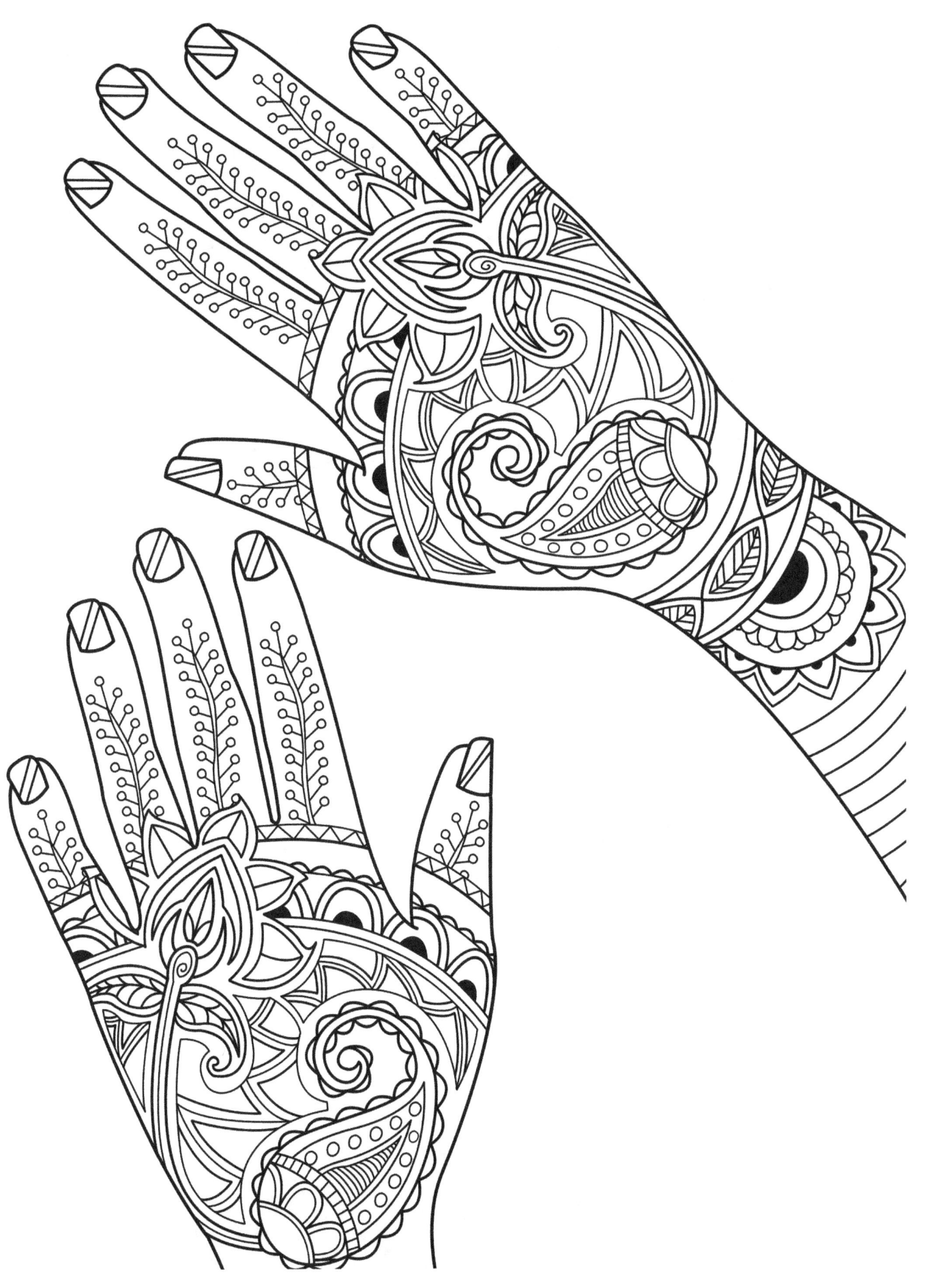

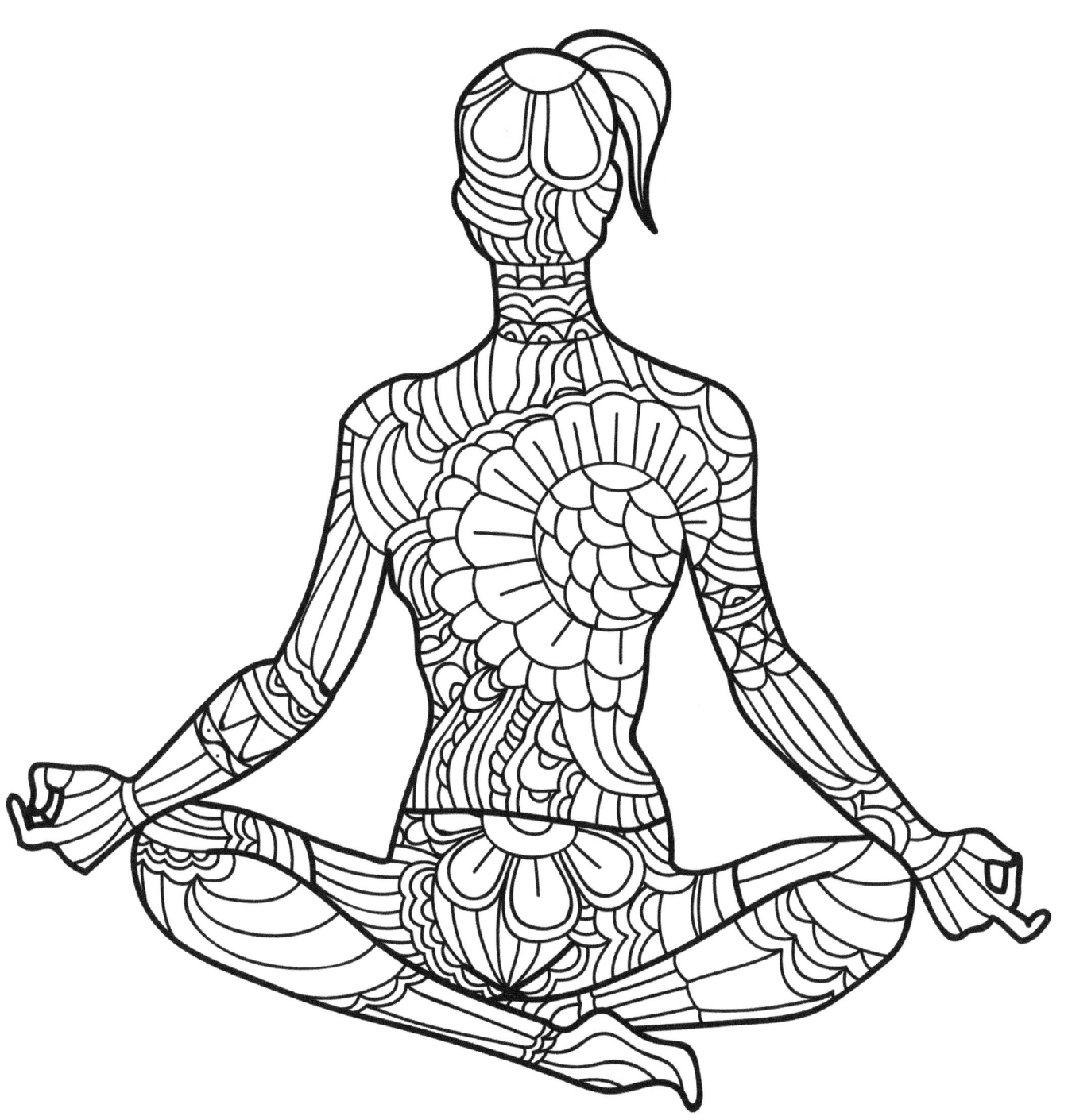

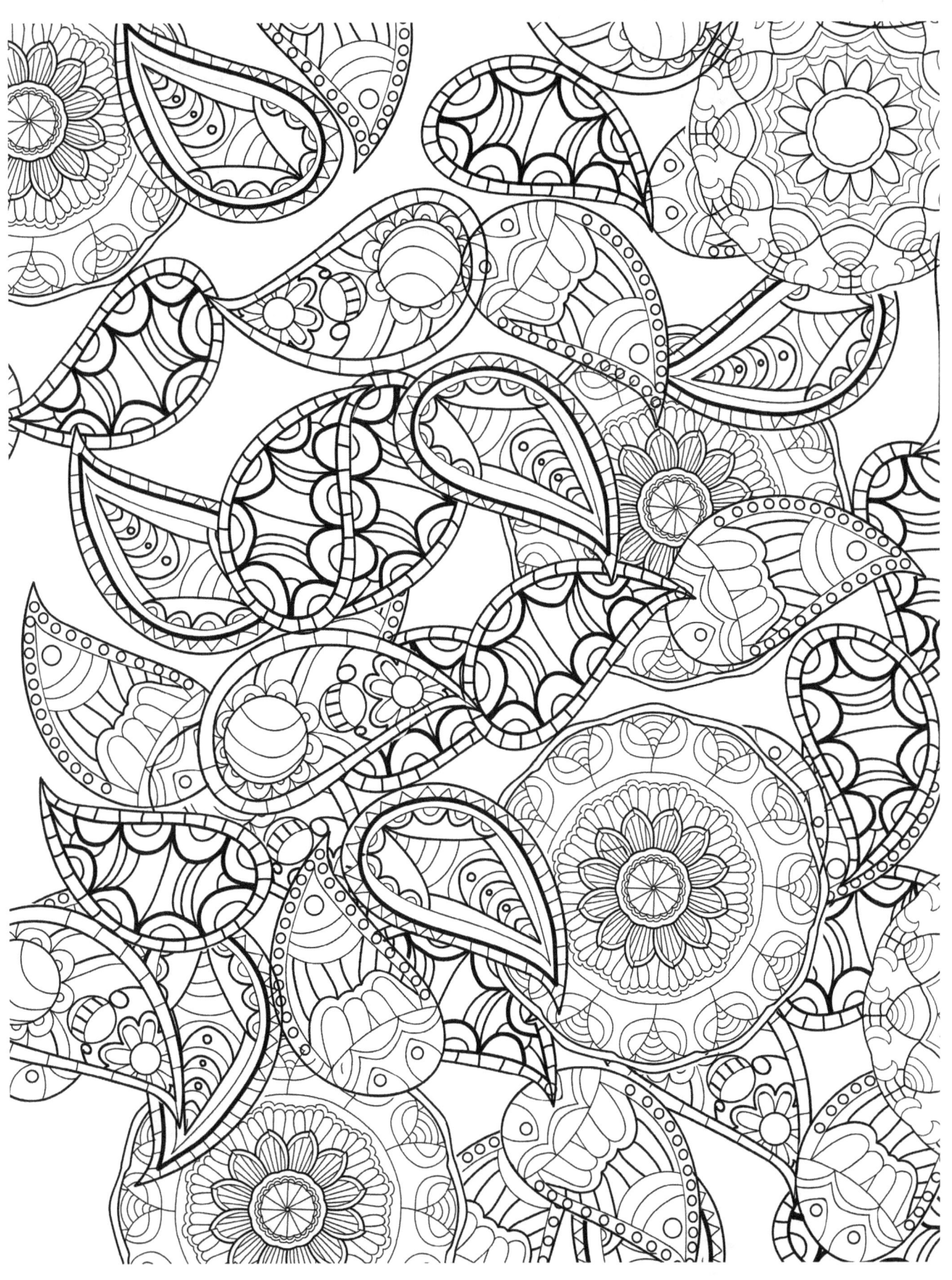

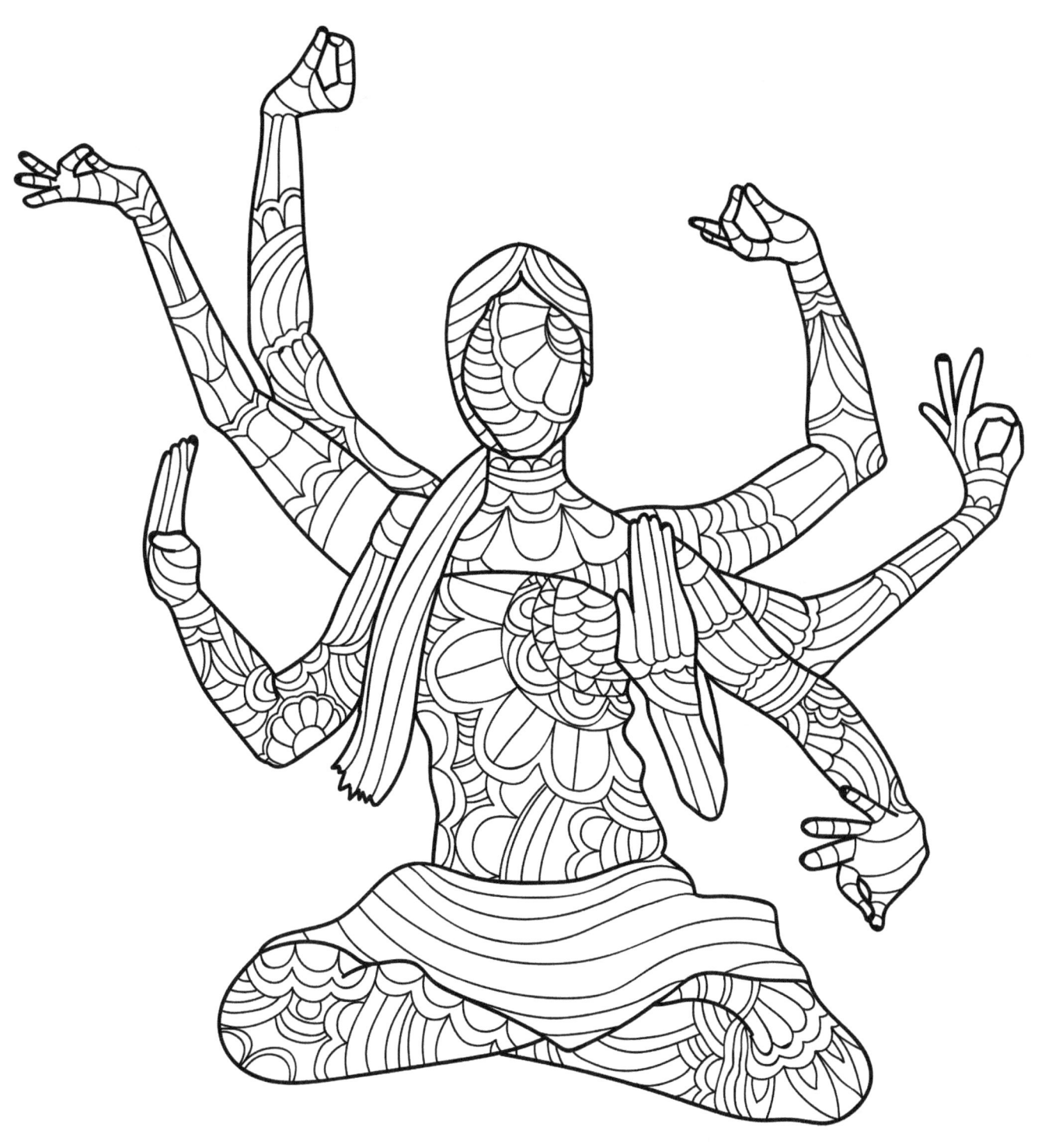

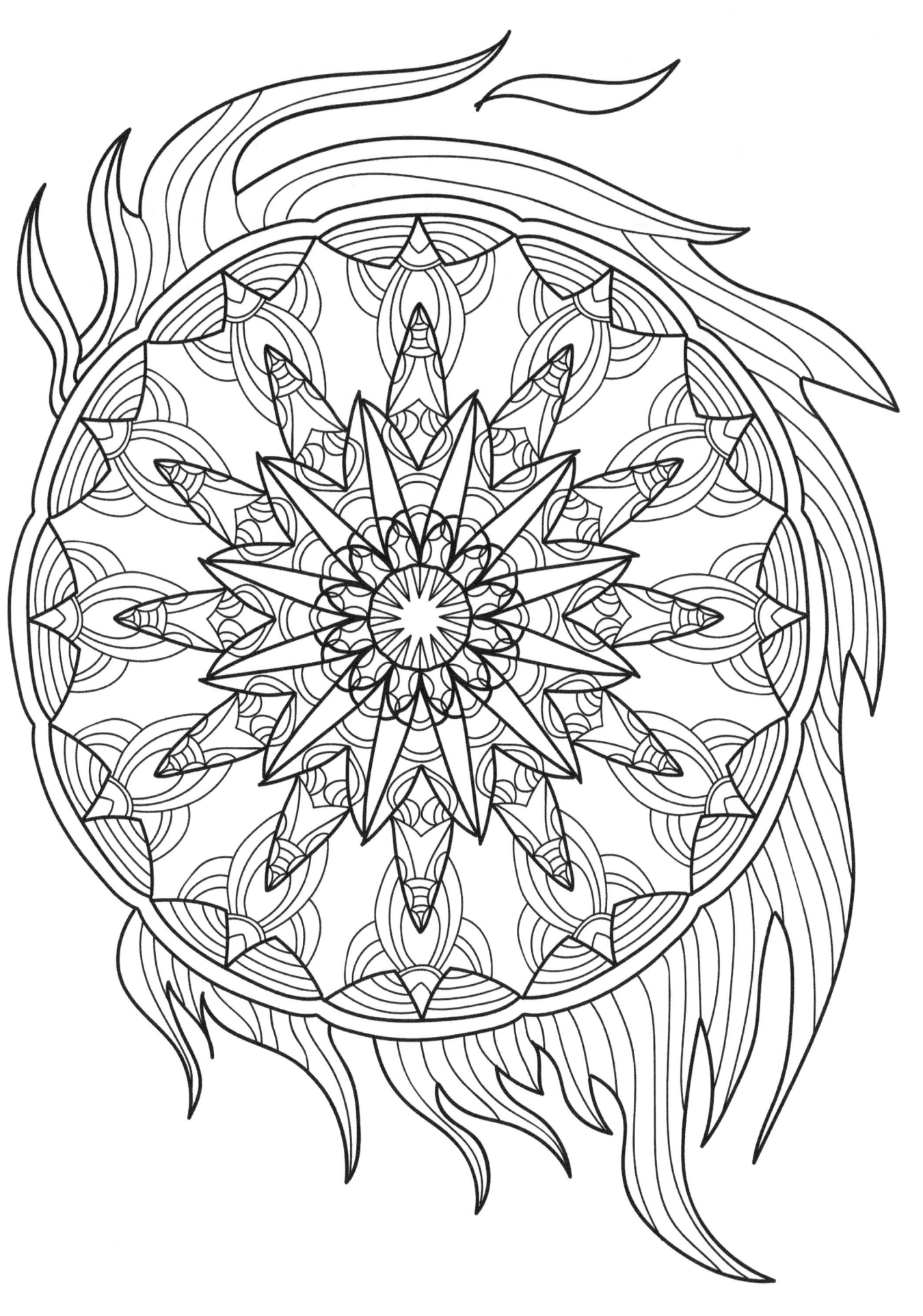

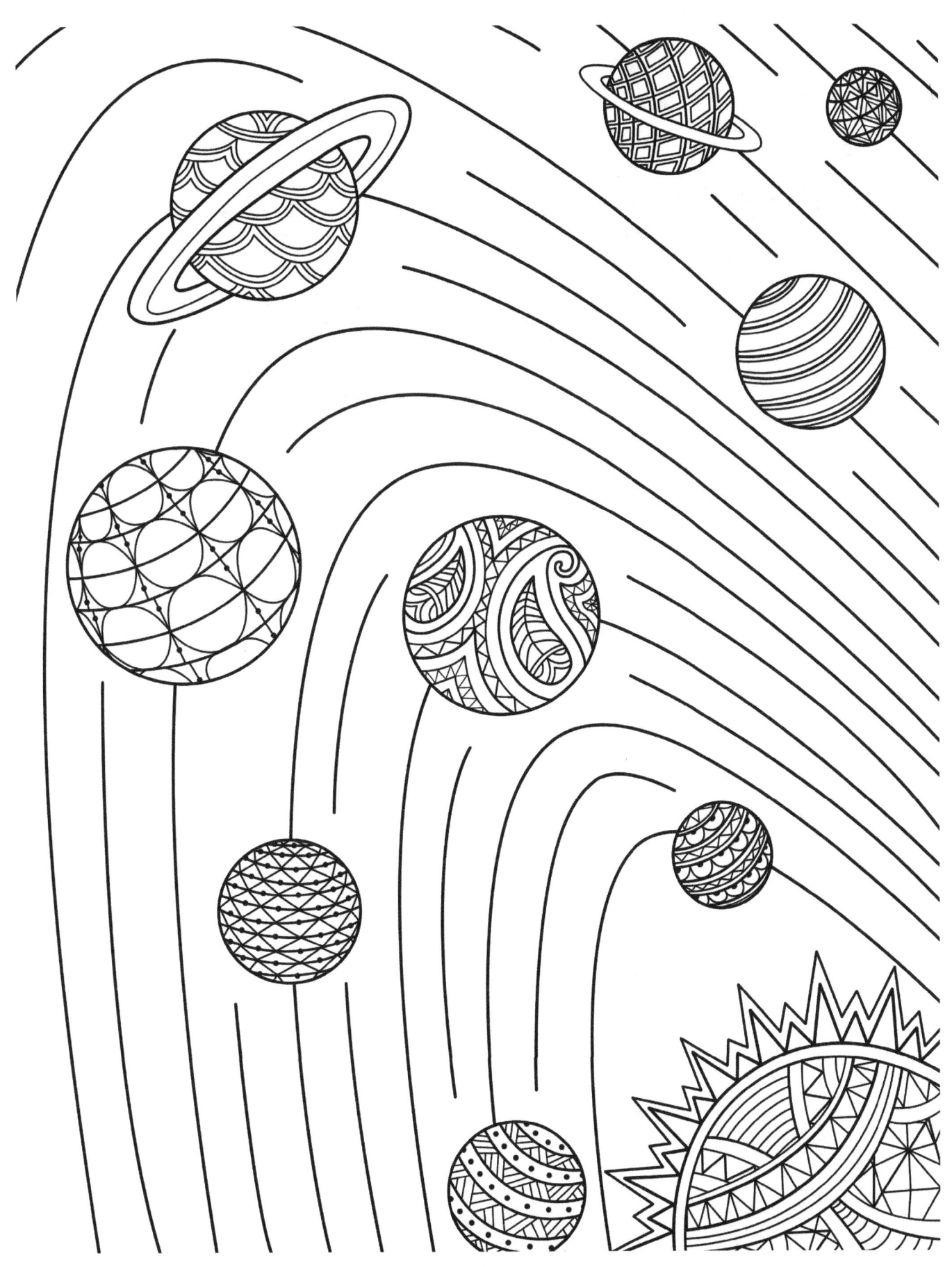

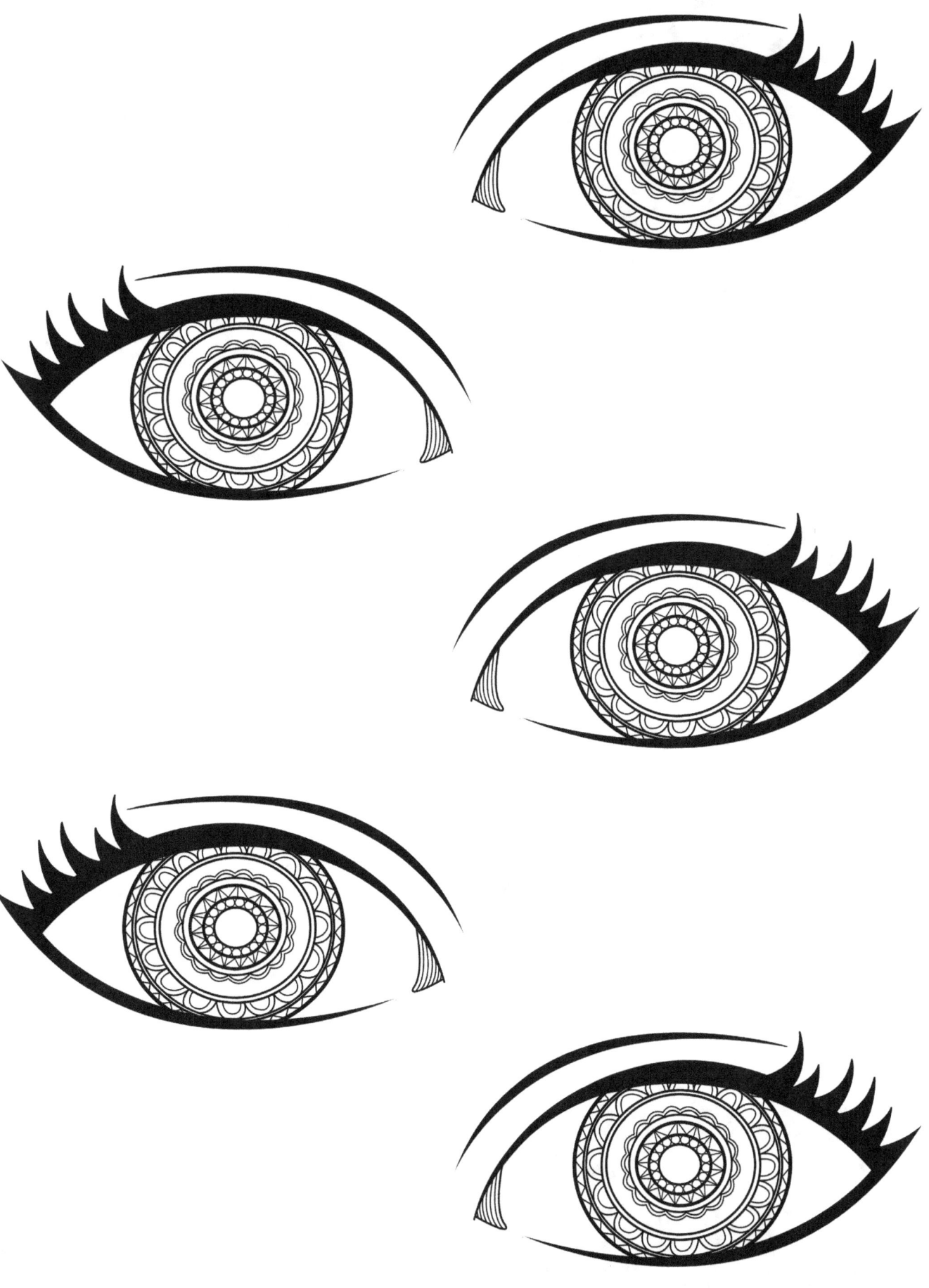

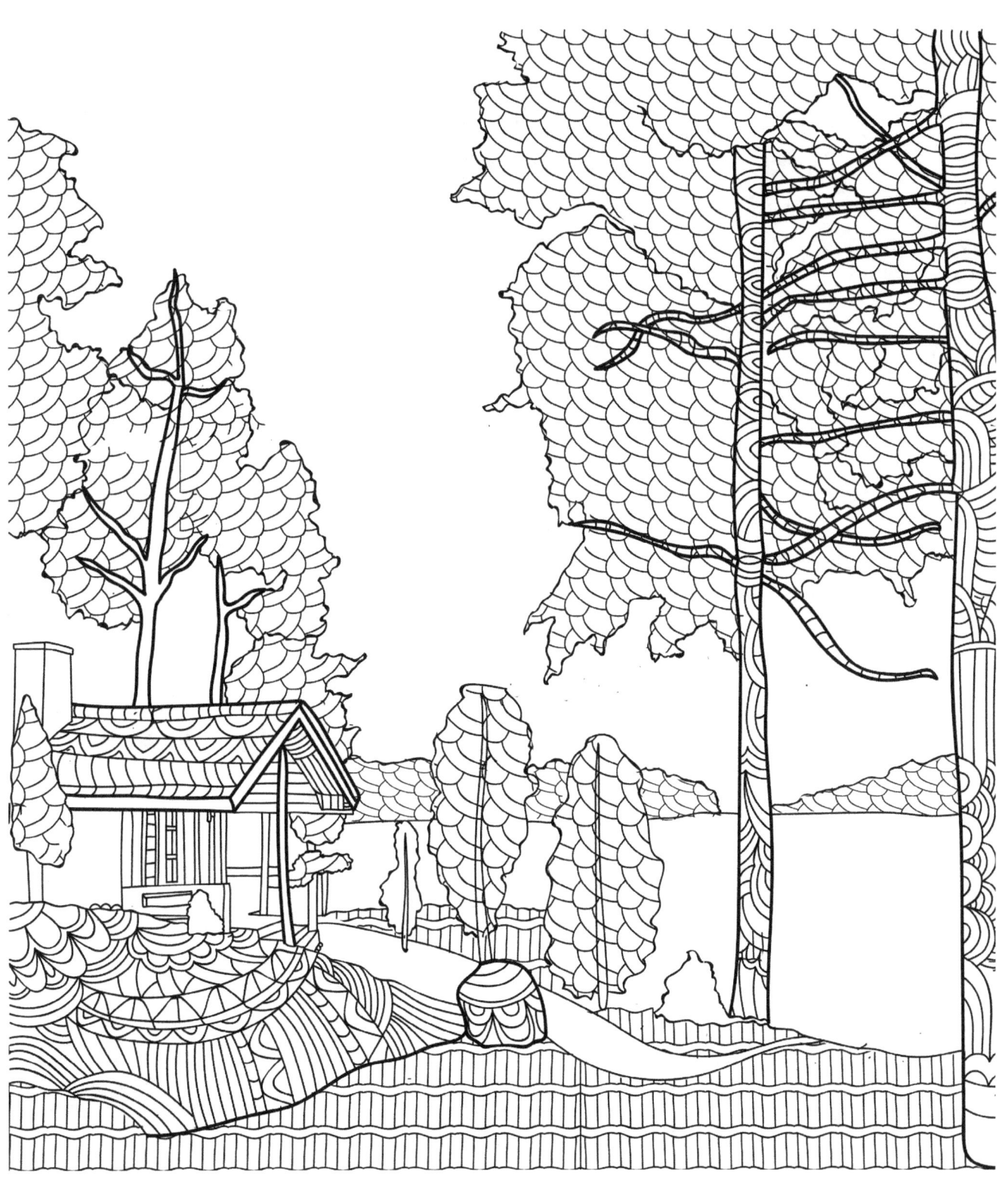

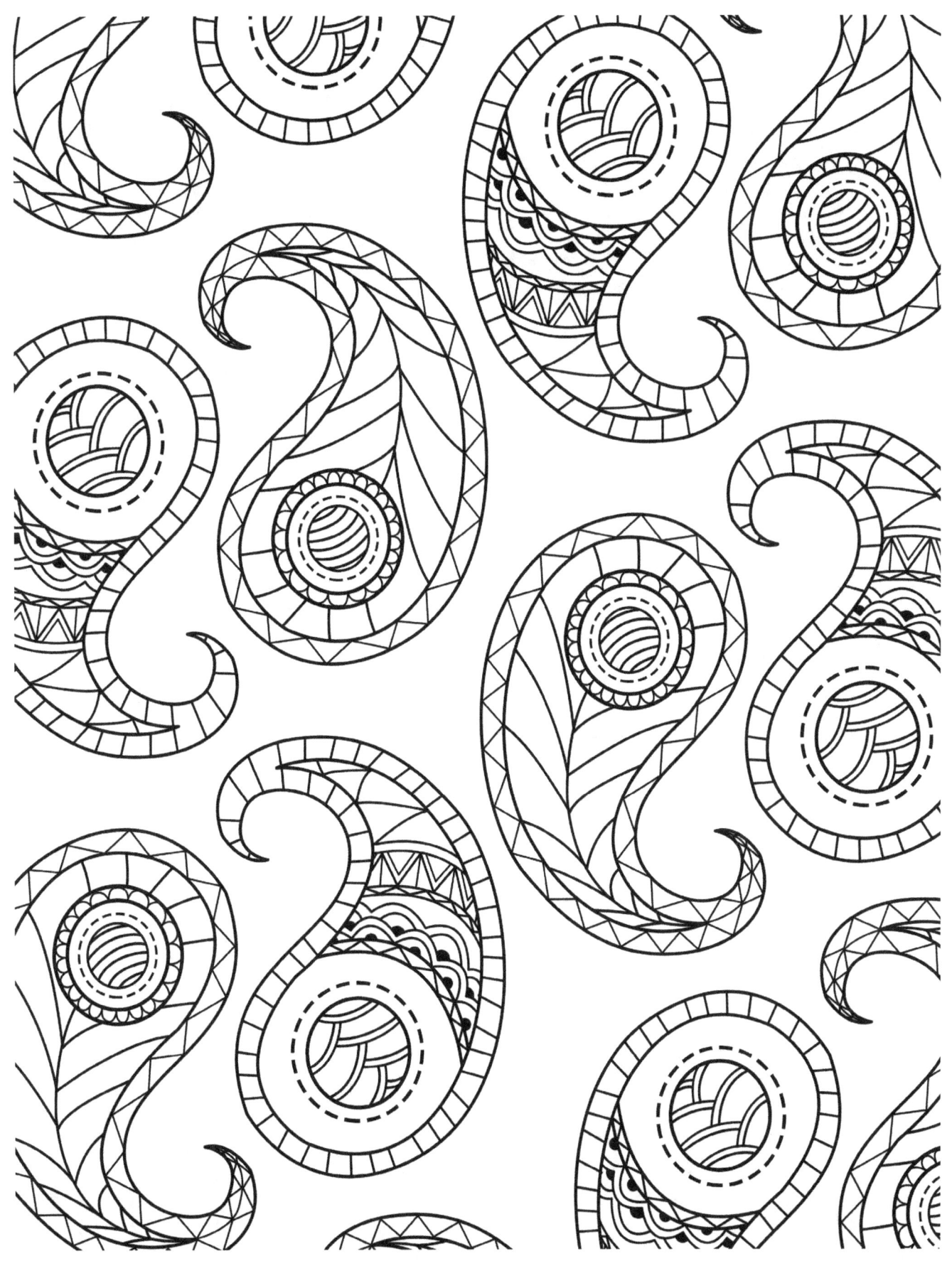

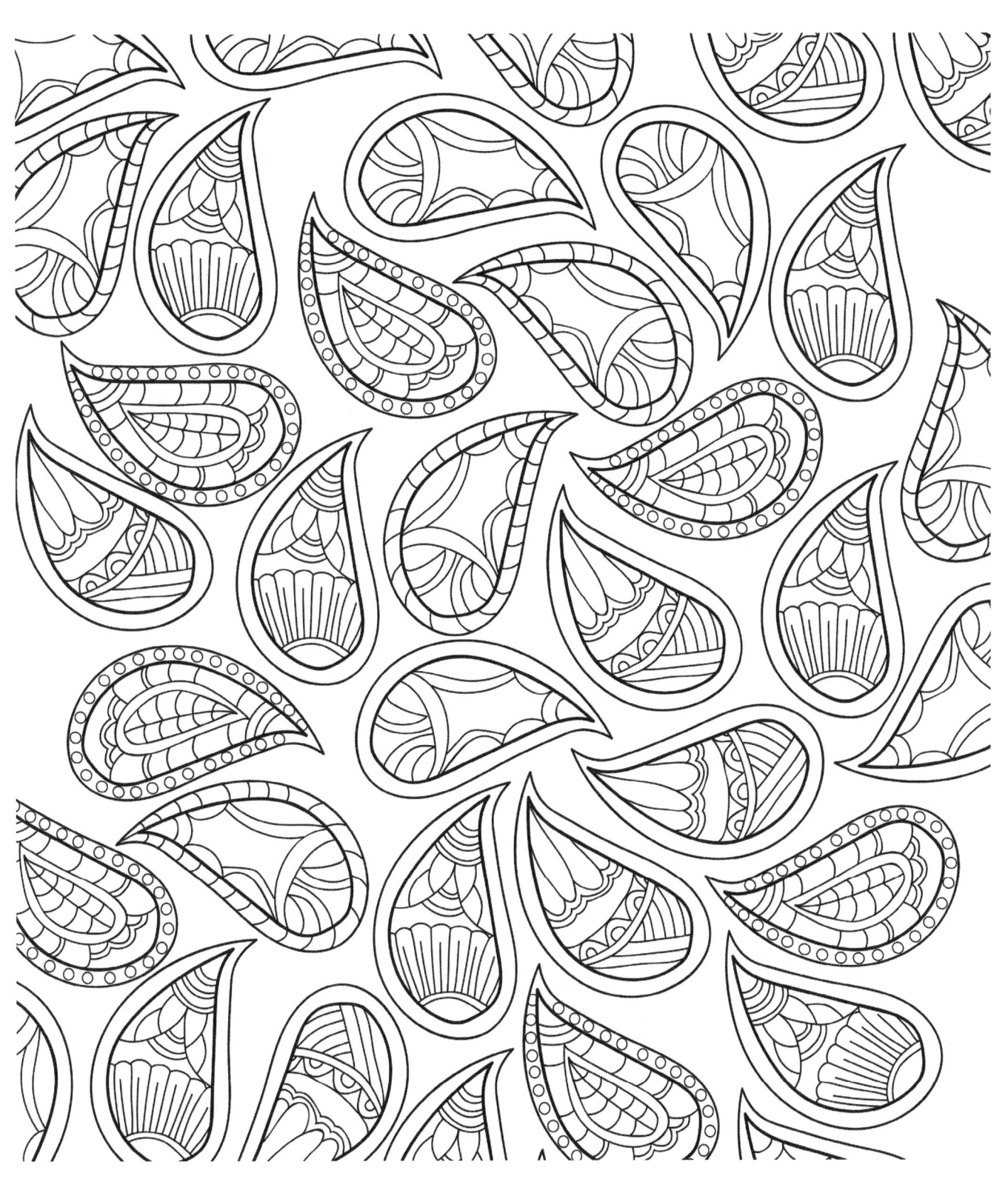

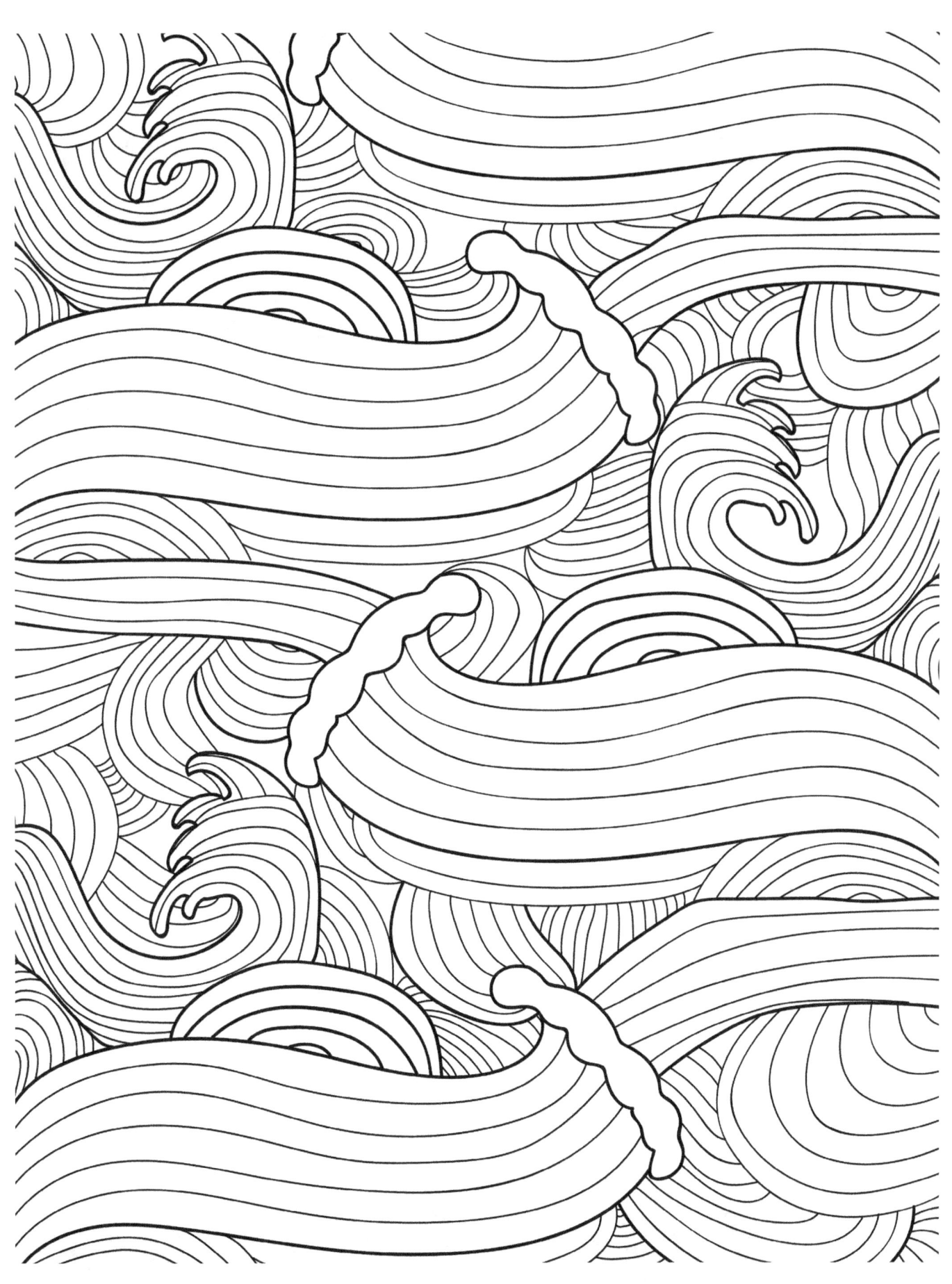

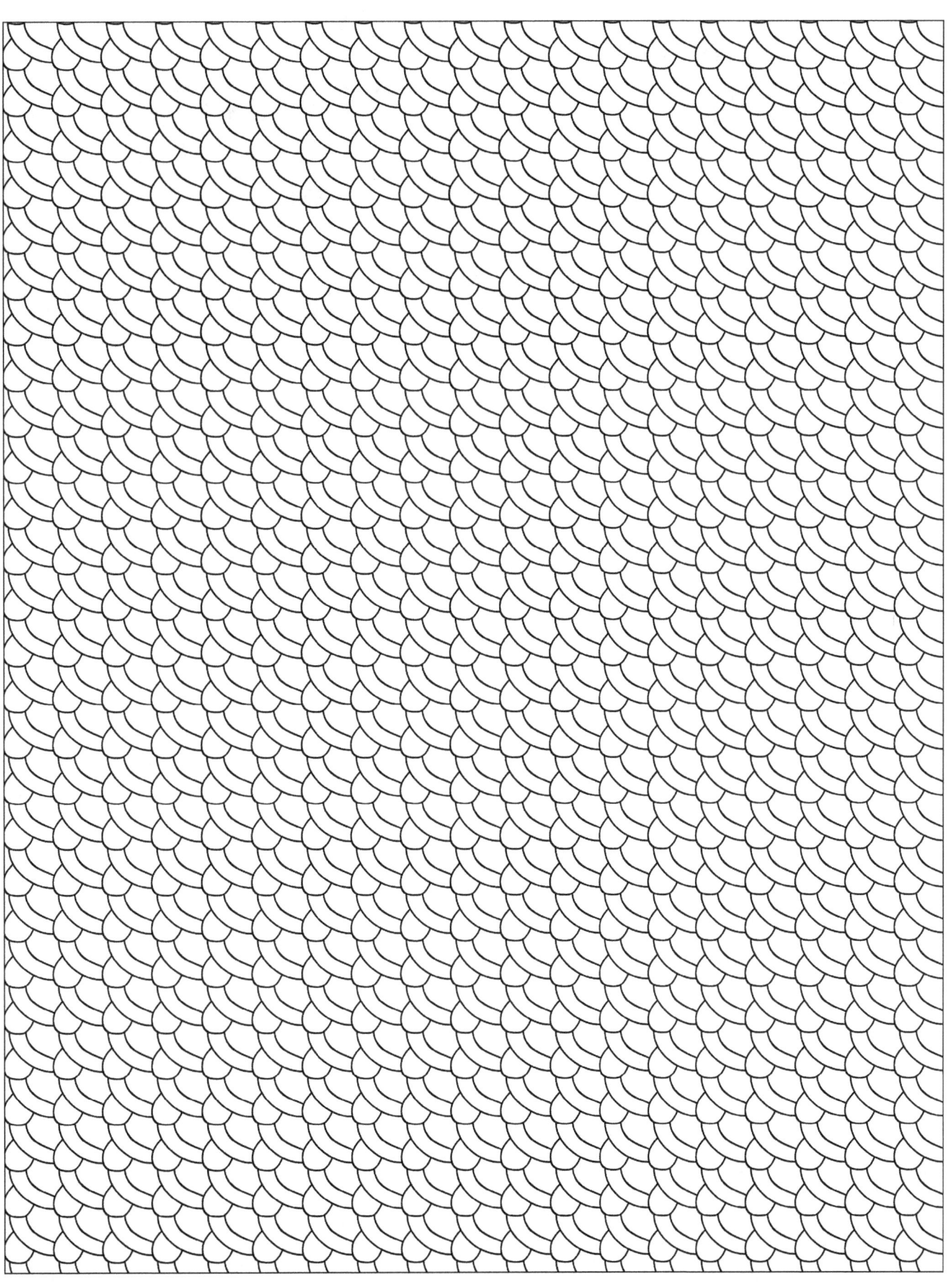

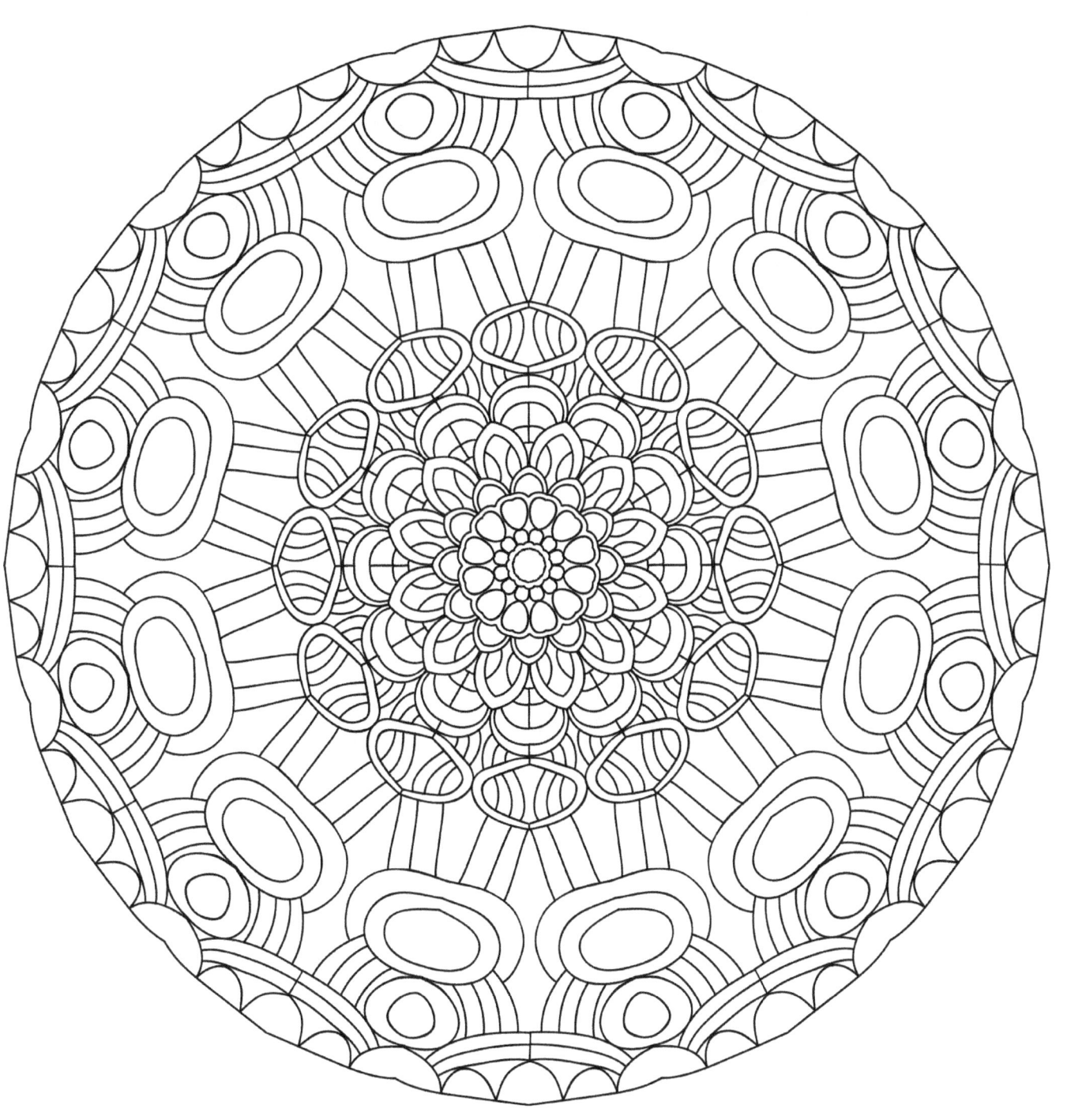

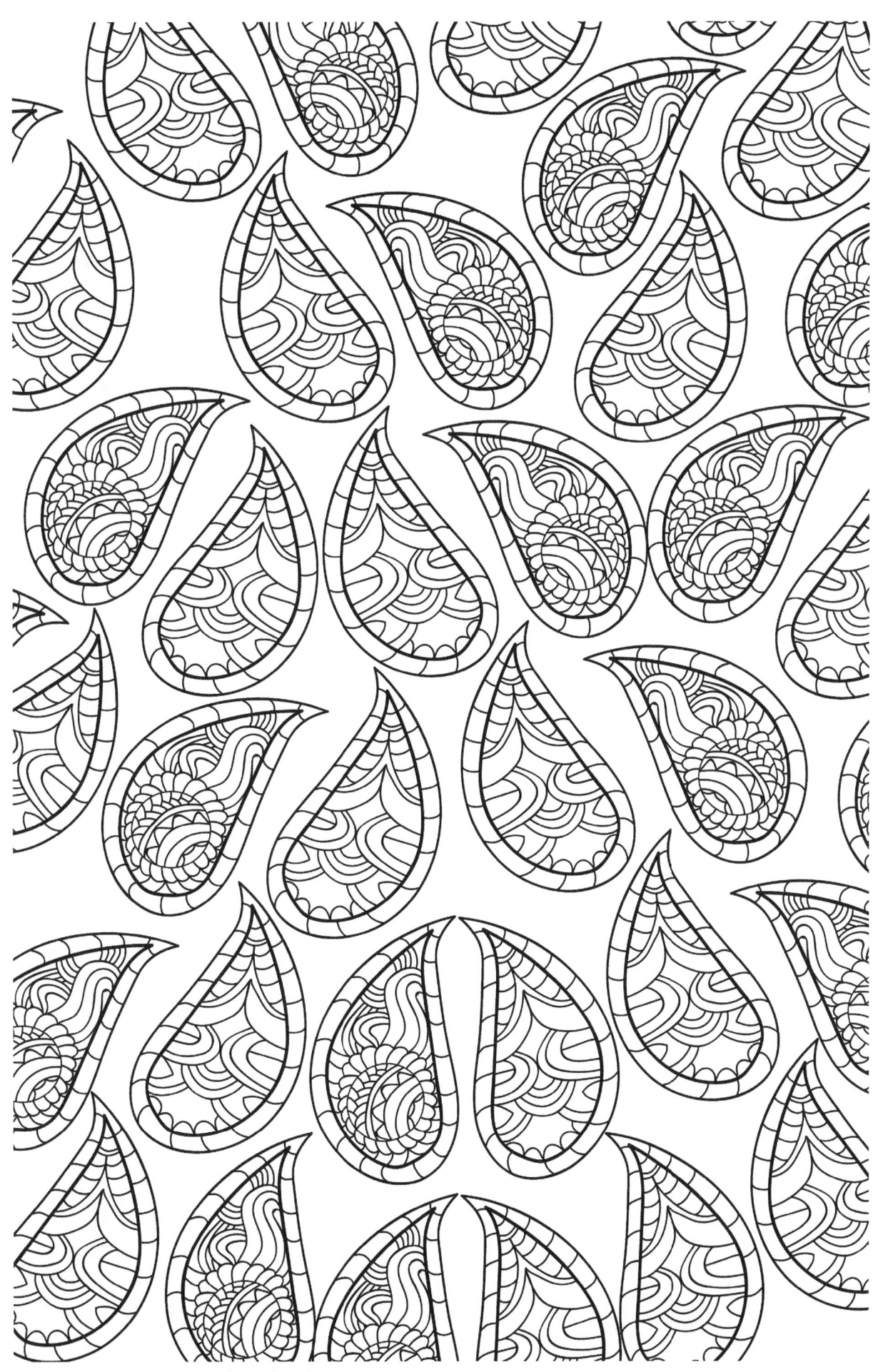

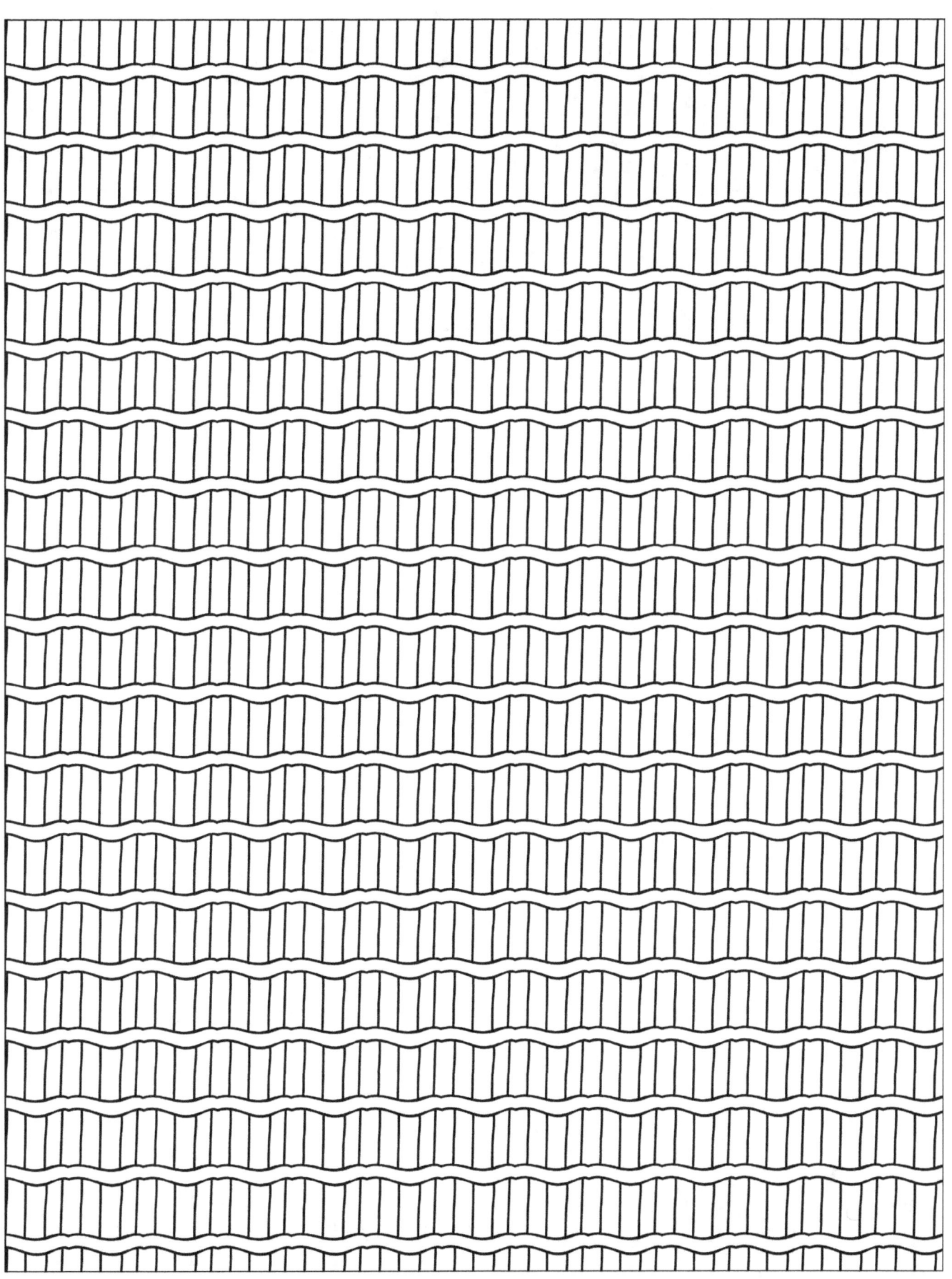

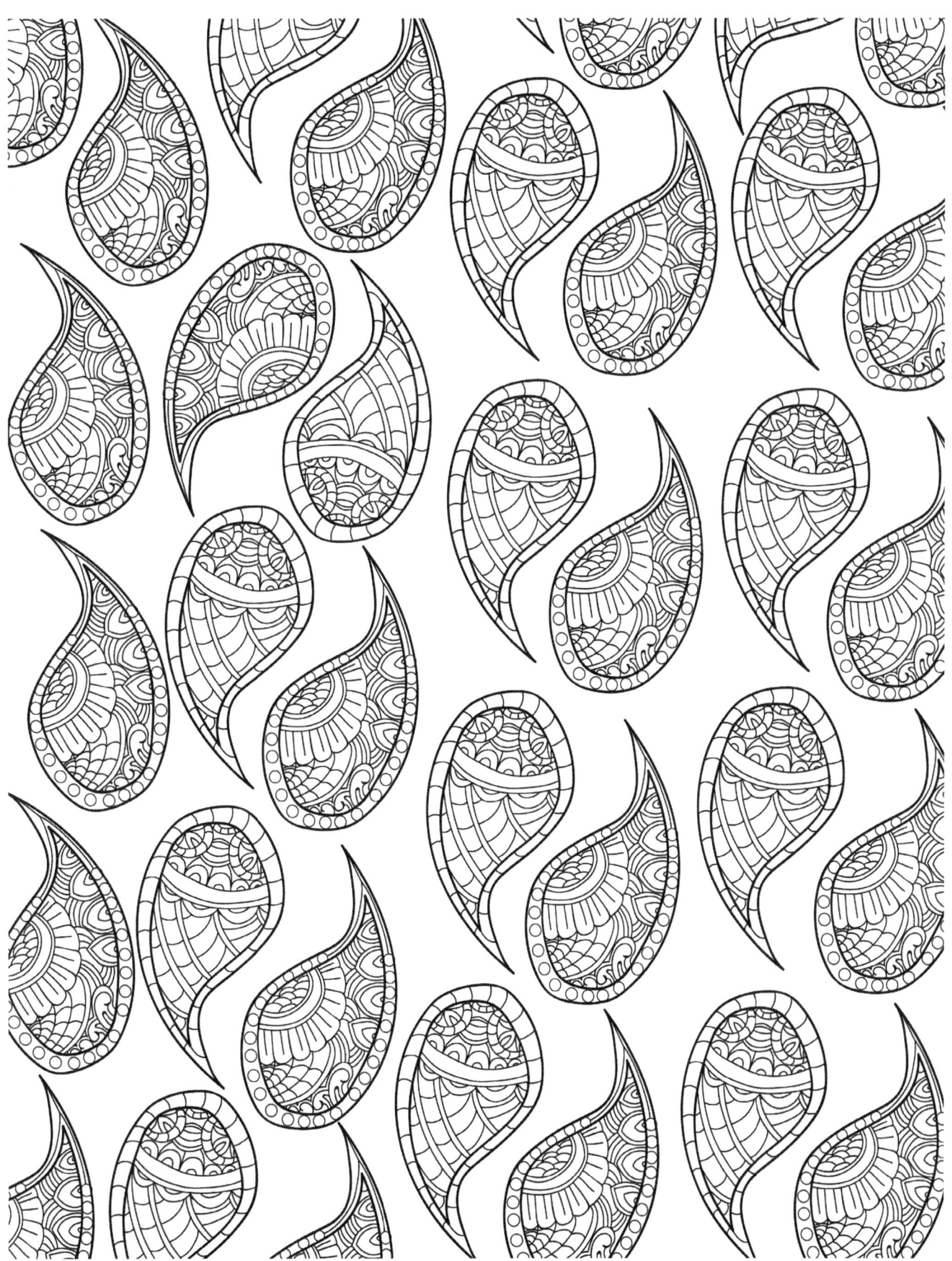

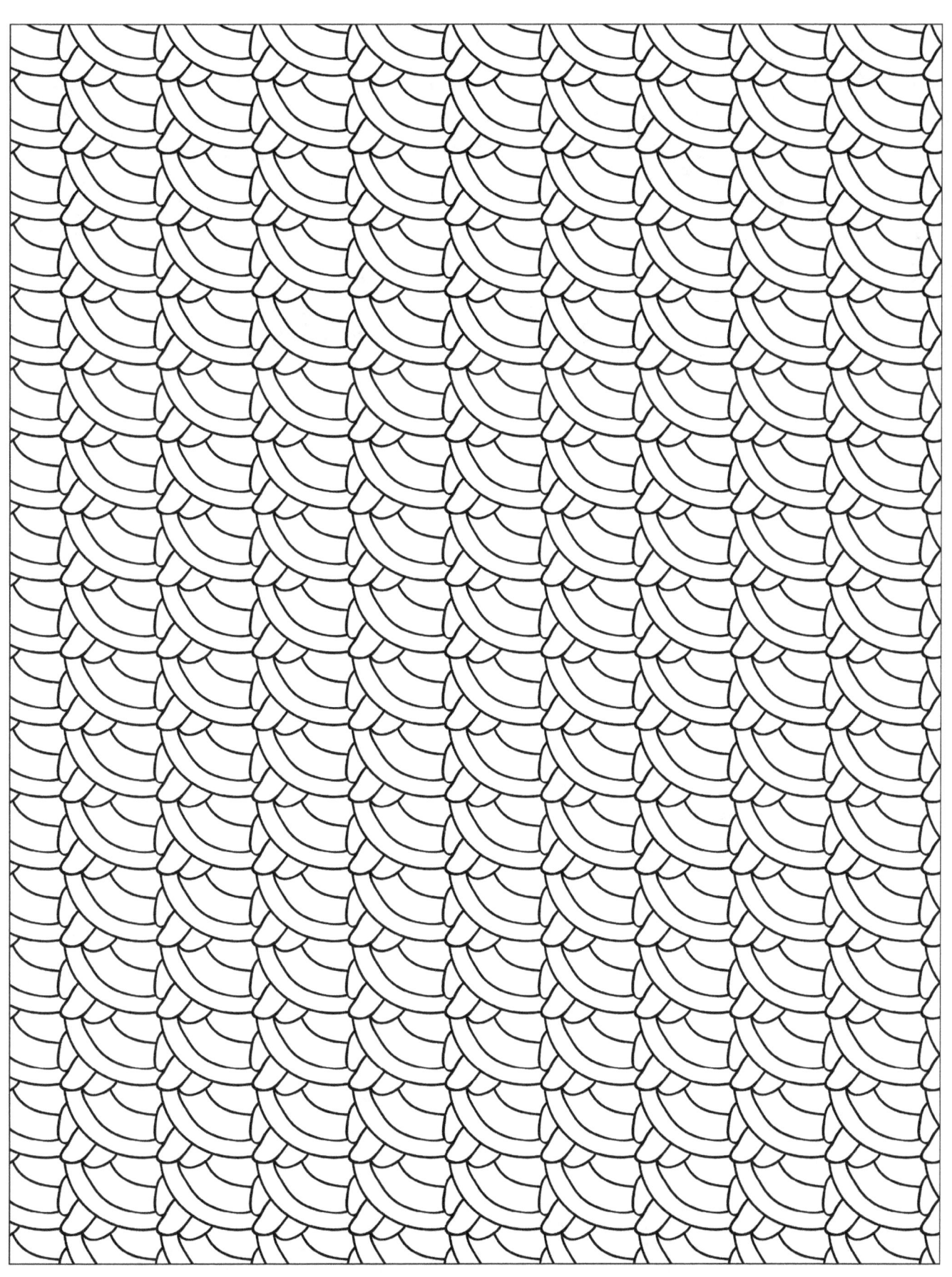

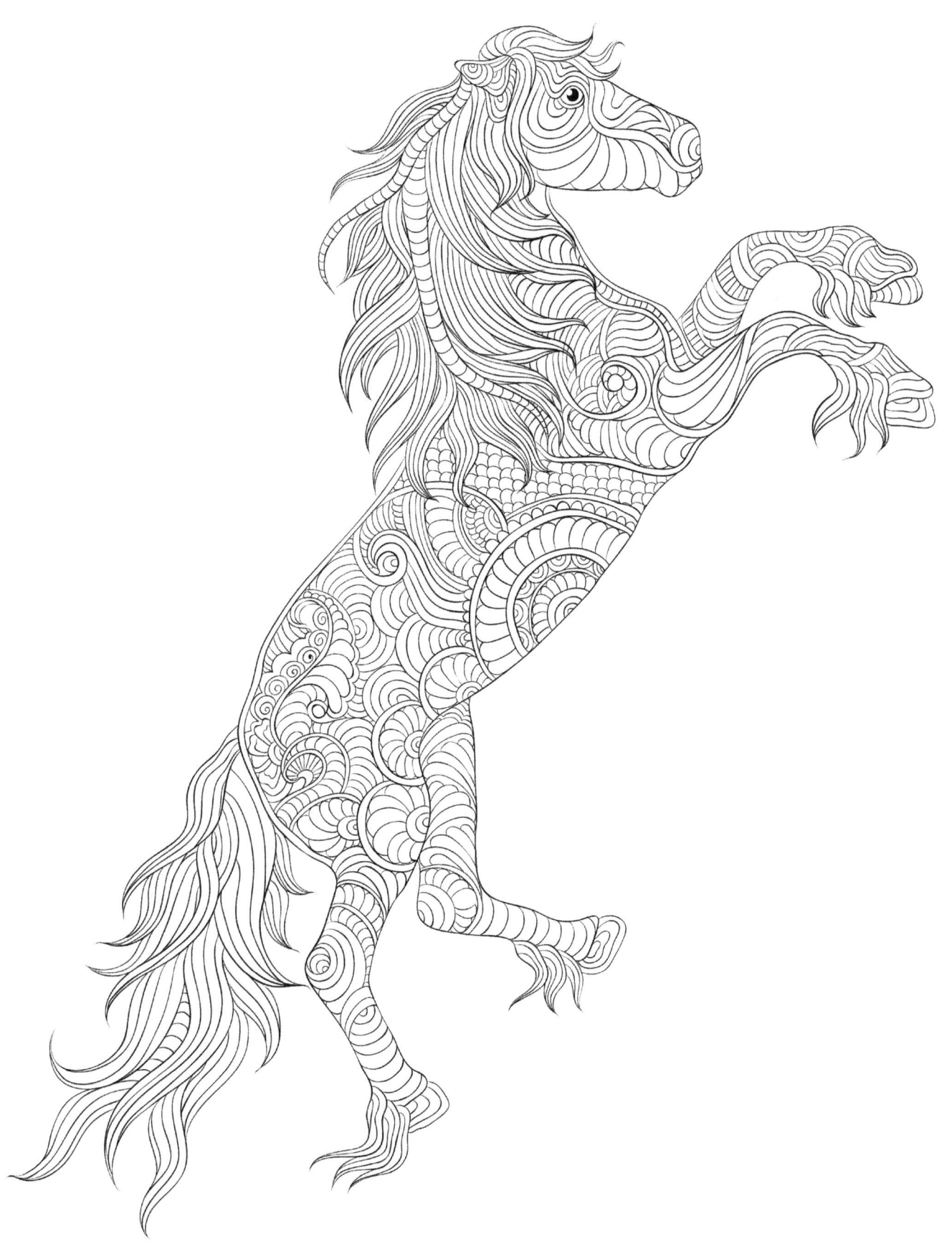

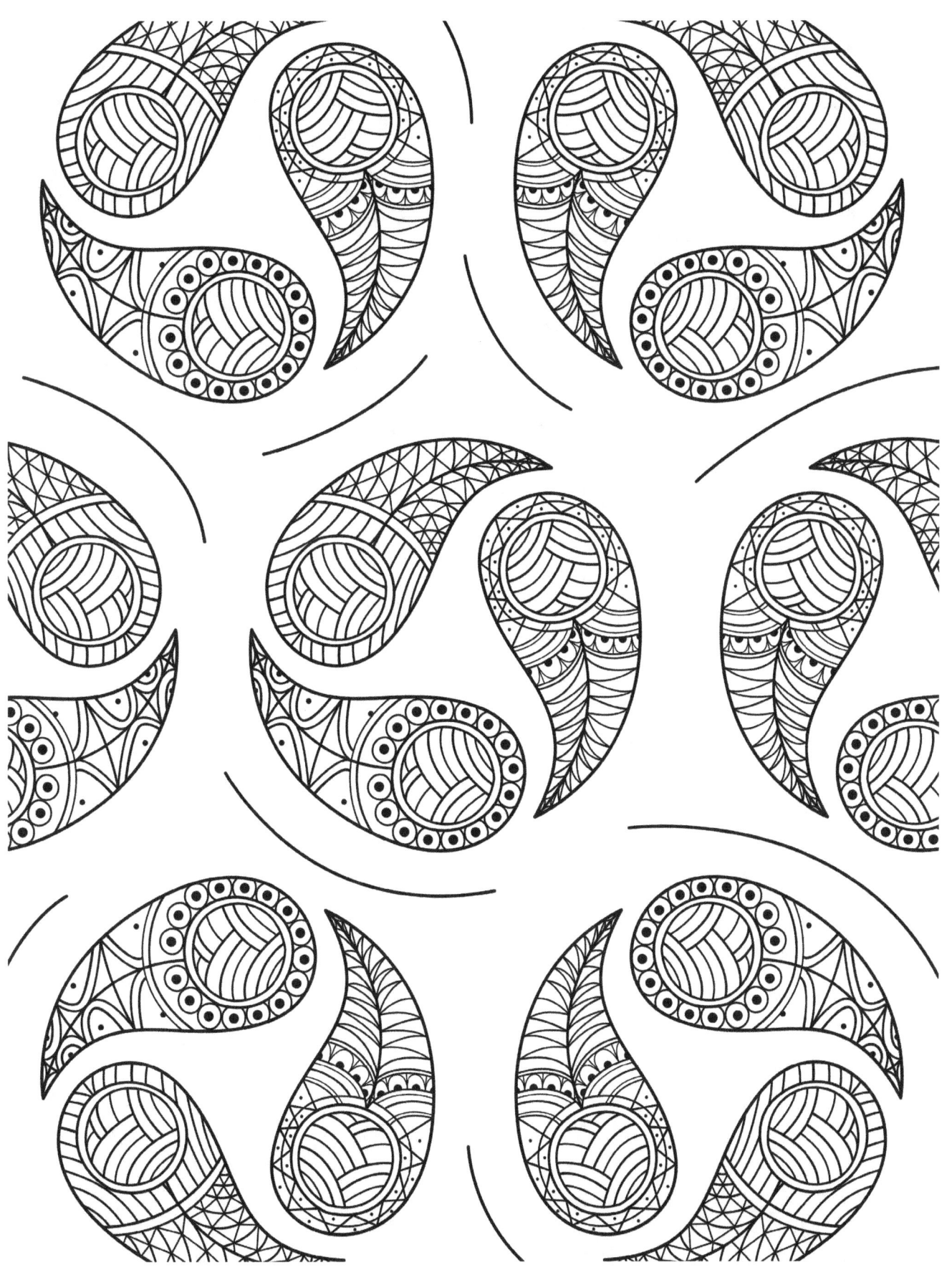

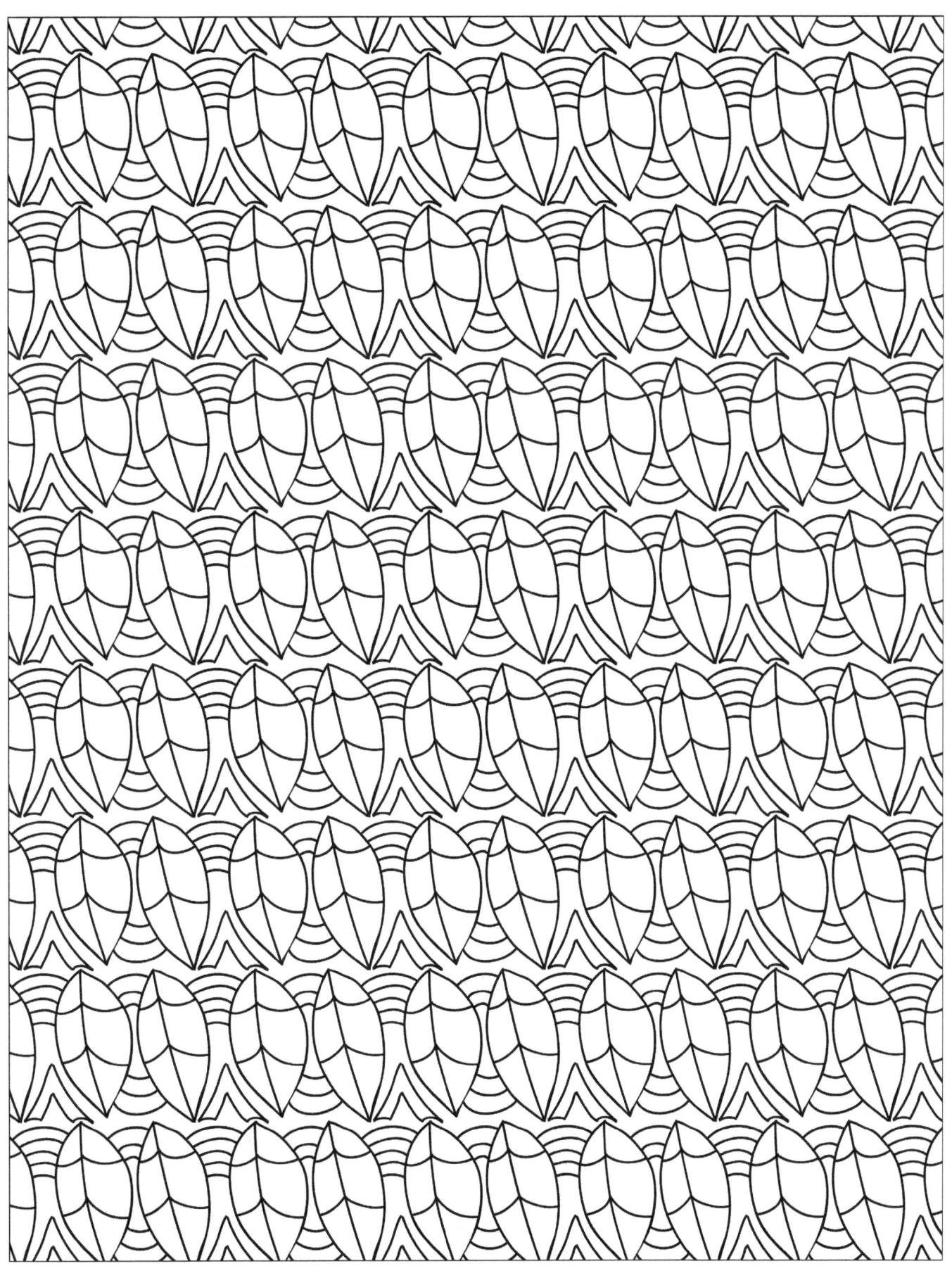

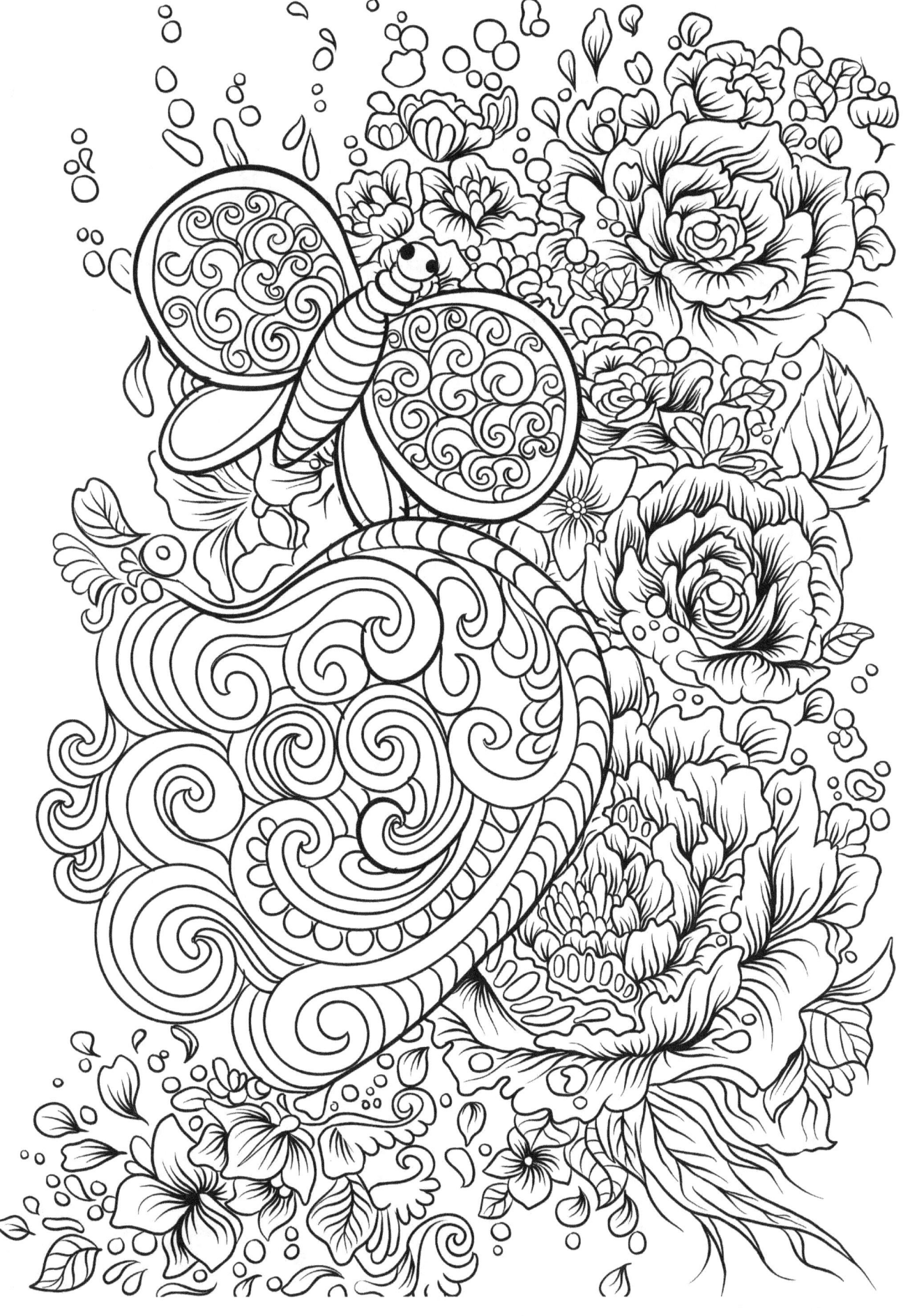

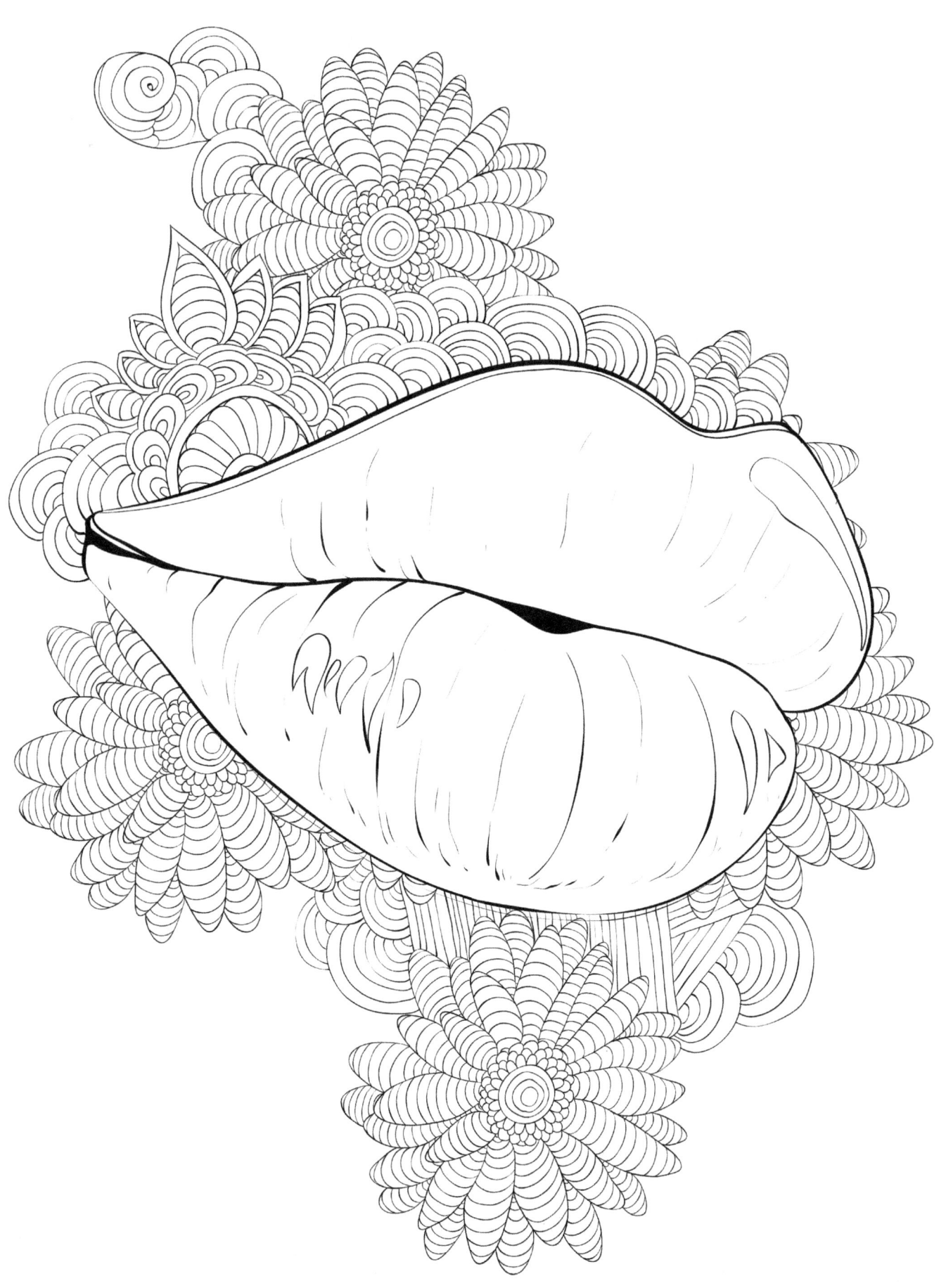

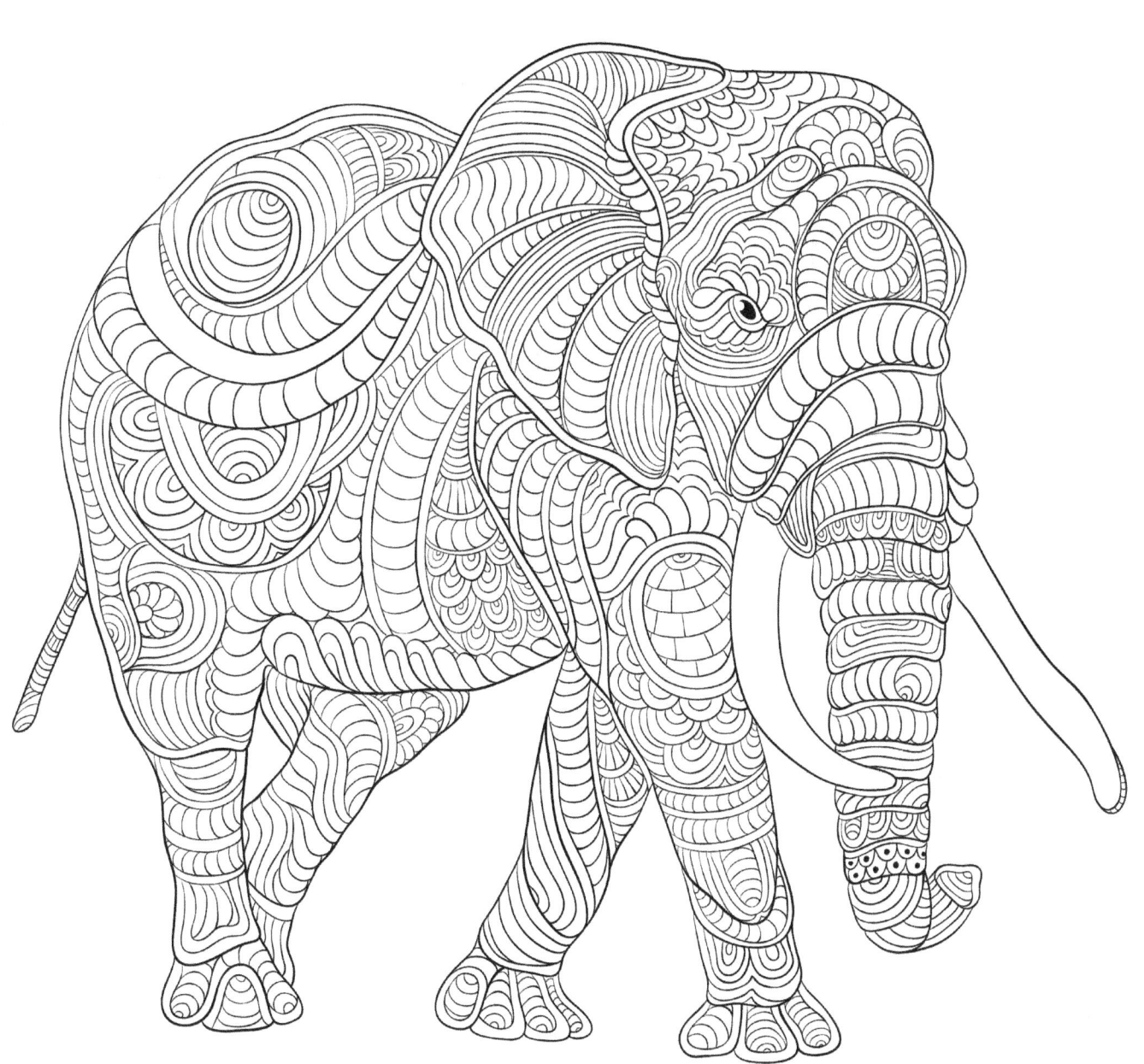

Free Bonus Book

$3.99 value electronic coloring book, easy to print out. Download your FREE book now:

http://CoolAdultColoringBooks.com

More: Check our website above for new books and special promotion deals…